ROBERT TOLF'S

Destination Florida

Sanibel &
Captiva
Islands

Other books by Robert Tolf
in the *Destination Florida* series

South Beach, Miami
Orlando's International Drive

ROBERT TOLF'S
Destination Florida

SANIBEL
& CAPTIVA
ISLANDS

TRIBUNE
PUBLISHING

Orlando / 1993

917.59
T57S

Copyright © 1993
Tribune Publishing
75 East Amelia Street
Orlando, Florida 32801

All rights reserved.

Series Editor: Dixie Kasper
Editor: Deborah Kane Mitchell
Text and jacket designer:
   Joy Dickinson
Text illustrations
   by Franklin Ayers
Cover illustration
   by Larry Moore

TRIBUNE PUBLISHING

Editorial Director:
   George C. Biggers III
Managing Editor: Dixie Kasper
Senior Editor: Kathleen M. Kiely
Production Manager: Ken Paskman
Designers: Bill Henderson,
   Eileen M. Schechner,
   Joy Dickinson

For information:
Tribune Publishing
P.O. BOX 1100
Orlando, Florida 32802

Printed in the United States

FIRST EDITION

Library of Congress Cataloging-in-Publication Data

Tolf, Robert W.
   Sanibel & Captiva Islands. — 1st ed.
   p.   cm. — (Robert Tolf's destination Florida)
   Includes index.
   ISBN 1-56943-001-2
   1. Sanibel Island (Fla.) — Guidebooks.   2. Captiva
Island (Fla.) — Guidebooks.   I. Title.   II. Title: Sanibel
and Captiva Islands.   III. Series: Tolf, Robert W.
Robert Tolf's destination Florida.
F317.S37T65   1993
917.59'48—dc20   93-30400
                                                            CIP

Contents

How to Use This Guide

DESTINATION FLORIDA GUIDEBOOKS ARE WRITTEN for discriminating, eager-to-learn, knowledgeable travelers — first-timers or repeats, one-day trippers, weekend warriors or extended escapees — all those who want to discover or rediscover what Florida has to offer. And it's a lot!

This book is organized into sections dealing with the basics, the where-to-eat and where-to-stay and what-to-see recommendations — only the best — along with practical information on shopping, surfing, souvenir hunting and the necessities — where to find a dry cleaner, photo shop, barber or hairdresser, limo or taxi.

"Fun in the Sun" listings include a wide range of bicycle, moped, boat and water sport equipment rentals, plus bait and tackle shops and the best places to find experienced guides to take you where the big ones are lurking or where the shelling is best.

Bookstores, newsstands and libraries are listed as are business services for those who want to keep their offices posted while vacationing. Museums are listed for those who want to learn about the culture and history of the area, art galleries for inside strolling and nature trails for outside treks. Those looking for a little night music will find separate listings of lounges with live entertainment, nightclubs, movies, concert halls and theaters.

We have not listed large supermarket and hardware store chains because, if you need their services, they are easy to find when you reach your destination.

The specific prices of accommodations and restaurants are not listed, but we have established the following general cost categories for double-occupancy rooms, and dinner for one including appetizer, main course, dessert and beverage, but not including tax, tip or drinks.

INEXPENSIVE Less than $15 for dinner for one. Less than $50 for a double-occupancy room.

MODERATE $15 to $30 for dinner for one. $50 to $125 for a double-occupancy room.

EXPENSIVE More than $30 for dinner for one. More than $125 for a double-occupancy room.

Many restaurants offer savings for the diners who like to eat early, the so-called early birds, and almost all of the accommodations offer seasonal savings from May through December, except in North Florida where the off-season runs from Labor Day to Memorial Day. There are also a great variety of package deals at these accommodations with terrific savings and all kinds of extras, so be sure to inquire when you call for reservations.

No complimentary lodging, meals, or other considerations and freebies were received in the research and gathering of information for this book.

How to Get Here

Sanibel-Captiva is 18 miles from the Fort Myers Southwest Regional Airport. From there, or from Exit 21 of Interstate 75, take Daniels Road west, crossing U.S. Highway 41 to continue on Summerlin Road—State Road 869—leading to the Sanibel Causeway and the tollbooth.

Tourist Information

Lee County Alliance of the Arts,
10091 McGregor Boulevard,
Fort Myers, FL 33919.
(813) 939-2787.

The Lee County Visitor and Convention Bureau, 2180 West First Street, #100, P.O. Box 2445, Fort Myers, FL 33902-2445. (813) 335-2631; toll-free in Florida: 1-800-237-6444; outside Florida: 1-800-LEE-ISLE (533-4753).

Sanibel-Captiva Chamber of Commerce, Causeway Road, P. O. Box 166, Sanibel, FL 33957. (813) 472-1080.

TV-39, Visitors TV, gives capsule video information on the islands' history, wilderness areas and refuges, restaurants, shopping and entertainment. Tune in AM Radio 1610 for information on the J. N. "Ding" Darling Wildlife Refuge.

Sanibel &
Captiva
Islands

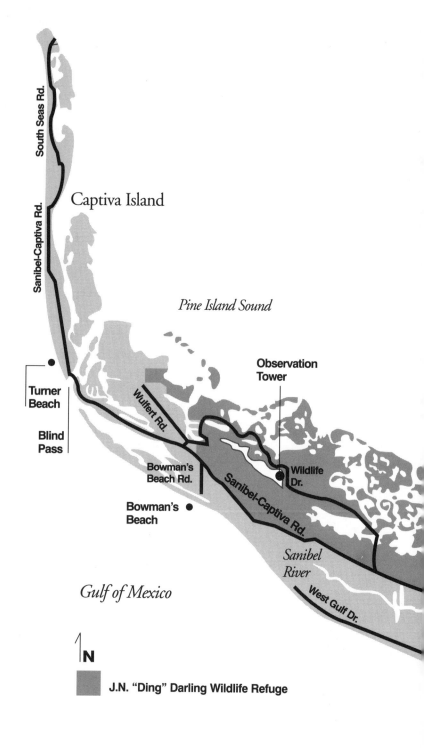

South Seas Rd.

Sanibel-Captiva Rd.

Captiva Island

Pine Island Sound

Observation
Tower

Turner
Beach

Blind
Pass

Wulfert Rd.

Bowman's
Beach Rd.

Bowman's
Beach

Wildlife
Dr.

Sanibel-Captiva Rd.

Sanibel
River

Gulf of Mexico

West Gulf Dr.

N

J.N. "Ding" Darling Wildlife Refuge

Sanibel &
Captiva Islands

Scale of Miles

0   1

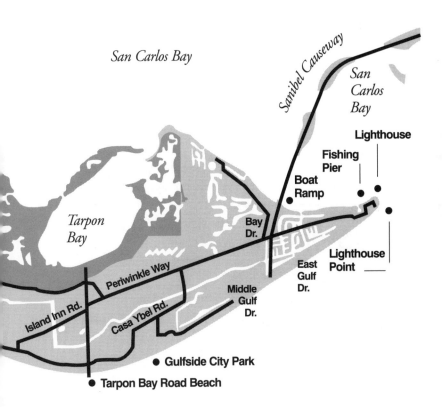

San Carlos Bay

Sanibel Causeway

San Carlos Bay

Lighthouse

Fishing
Pier

Boat
Ramp

Tarpon Bay

Bay
Dr.

Lighthouse
Point

Periwinkle Way

East
Gulf
Dr.

Island Inn Rd.

Casa Ybel Rd.

Middle
Gulf
Dr.

● Gulfside City Park

● Tarpon Bay Road Beach

Welcome to Sanibel & Captiva!

THE ADVENTURE, THE ESCAPE, THE RETREAT FROM mainland realities, begin as soon as you leave the tollbooth and look down the ribbon of stone and asphalt leading to the island getaways of Sanibel and Captiva.

Don't rush it. Stop and look, and then look some more. Pull over to the side of the causeway and survey the scene. Off to your left, to the east, you can see the lighthouse, a soaring 98-foot sentinel constructed more than a century ago, in 1884, as a warning beacon to ships navigating around a dangerous sandbar in San Carlos Bay. Unlike the bandits of Key West, who never wanted a lighthouse so they could continue to salvage the wrecks rounding the Keys, the few pioneering residents of these islands did not prosper from others' misfortunes — with the mosquitoes, heat and humidity they had enough of their own. Sanibel holds the world's record for the greatest concentration of mosquitoes — in the days before mosquito control and abatement.

The Sanibel lighthouse guided the early settlers to their new island adventure.

Ferries, freighters, mail and fishing boats provided the only links to the mainland, chiefly the point of flat land named by the Spaniards Punta Rassa, U.S. terminal of the International Ocean Telegraph Company's cable to Cuba from the late 19th century until 1936. It was the transshipment port for cattle being sent for sale to Cuba and the Bahamas, thousands of them from Central Florida ranges — $6 a steer, $3 to ship, and sold for $15 or $20.

Herders and drovers rounded up range cattle, descendants of those first animals introduced to their New World by the Spanish. They were put in Punta Rassa pens built by one of Florida's first millionaires, Jake Summerlin — the road you took on the mainland leading to the causeway honors his memory.

The Sanibel lighthouse kept the Cuba and Nassau-bound boats off the sandbar just as it guided the early settlers to their new island adventure. But they were not the first. The earliest residents on these islands, which are relatively young, only 5,000 years or so old, were the Calusa Indians. These Native Americans successfully resisted and repulsed the Spanish for years, starting with that legendary figure of early exploration, the conquistador who sailed with Columbus and who discovered Florida in 1513, Ponce de Leon. San Carlos Bay was named for the Calusas' crafty cacique, their chief, Carlos, who led his men against the explorer, frustrating his efforts to colonize the areas of Florida around Sanibel.

Contemplate that bloody history as you look across the causeway at the islands: Sanibel dead ahead, Pine Island off to the right, and to the north, Captiva and Upper Captiva across the Pine Island Sound. The low-lying stretches of sand form protective barriers shielding the mainland from the furies of the storms and those really Big Winds, which the natives called "Hurra-kan." Shorelines shift, passes fill with sand and shells, roads and trails wash away along the ever-changing coastlines. Upper Captiva was cast loose by a major storm in 1921 when Redfish Pass was opened between the two Captivas. The great hurricane five years later, which burst the bubbles of the South Florida real estate boom, widened the pass.

Captiva was where the notorious pirate, Jose Gaspar, who adopted the name Gasparilla, Little Gaspar, supposedly found safe haven, and where he secreted 11 beautiful Mexican maidens and a princess, giving the girls to his men and keeping the princess for himself. When she rejected his advances, off went her head and, lo and behold, the island where the remaining 11 were held prisoner was forevermore known as Captiva. Gasparilla was reputed to be a gentleman who read the classics, a diarist who recorded the capture of

Captiva Island was where the notorious pirate, Gasparilla, found safe haven.

three dozen ships and untold booty. A lovely legend, but the tales were told by a reputed brother-in-law, Juan Gomez, who lived on one of the Ten Thousand Islands south of Sanibel and supposedly lived to be 119 years old. Also, the name Captiva appears on nautical charts before Gasparilla's not-so-heroic exploits in the late 18th century.

Easier to document is the history of Captiva's first white settler. William Binder arrived the year after the Sanibel lighthouse

was lighted, the first year the island was brought into the national Homestead Act. The present-day Chapel by the Sea was built in 1901, originally to serve as a schoolhouse, on Binder's land, which also became the Captiva Cemetery. Binder is buried there.

The Dickeys of Virginia were Captiva's first winter residents, moving in about the time the inexhaustible Teddy Roosevelt discovered how great local waters were for deep-sea fishing. During one lengthy encounter, the President reportedly fought the entire day with a two-ton manta, a devilfish, that measured 30 feet across. Before he could beach the monster on a spit of sand in Blind Pass — ever after called Devilfish Key and Roosevelt Beach —

half a hundred steel-jacketed .50-caliber bullets had to be fired into its massive body.

You're not going to encounter anything quite so threatening while enjoying island waters today, but you will come across parades of palms and clumps of Key lime trees thanks to another pioneer. Clarence Chadwick planted row after row of palms to process for copra and coconut oil. Tomatoes and winter vegetables were other cash crops, and at one time, Chadwick's groves supplied fully 90 percent of the nation's supply of Key limes. The hurricanes of the 1920s, with impossible-to-stem saltwater intrusion, washed out the plantation's prosperity, and in the years before World War II, his buildings were converted to guest accommodations. Thirty years later a group of investors from Fort Myers, the Mariner Group, took over and the rest is history — the rest is South Seas Plantation.

There were other pioneering farmers, raising citrus and tropical fruits along with winter crops of tomatoes, cucumbers and various greens. And there were anglers who harvested the rich yields of surrounding Gulf and bay waters. Many of their homes went to sea over the years, floating and blowing away during the Big Winds, overwhelmed by the ceaseless ebb and flow of tidal incursions, the fury of crashing surf.

At one time, pioneer Clarence Chadwick's groves supplied 90 percent of the nation's supply of Key limes.

Many of the pioneers' homes went to sea over the years, floating and blowing away during the Big Winds.

You won't be driving on the causeway during such interruptions of tranquil island life, so pull over to the side of the road — there's plenty of free parking — and take a dip or cast a line. You'll be in good company with other waders and splashers, anglers and snorkelers, who seek the seductive solace of warm tropical waters blessed by a sun that never seems to stop shining.

From the tiniest crabs to the mighty tarpon, the waters conceal colonies and schools of sea creatures. The deep waters north of Captiva are the winter home of the tarpon, making Boca Grande Pass the Tarpon Fishing Headquarters of the World.

Sanibel-Captiva has one of the greatest concentrations of easy-to-recommend places to eat in the country.

If you can't go after those trophies, not to worry. There are plenty of other fish in the sea — cobia and grouper, redfish, snapper, sheepshead and trout — fish you can grill on your own gear and will find on the tables in the many restaurants that give Sanibel-Captiva one of the greatest concentrations of easy-to-recommend places to eat in the country.

You'll be swimming and fishing in the beautiful waters where pleasure boats now glide and splash past, where the mail boats and ferries used to transport their cargoes — residents and a few fortunate tourists, those not arriving in their own craft, laden with provisions for stays longer than a few hours or days.

Those boats were the lifeline before the land link was forged in 1963 — a date that remains infamous to all the old islanders who recall with regret and remorse when there were no paved roads, no condominiums and only a few hostelries.

Development is inevitable, but whether it can be controlled or not is up to the community. Florida, of all states, has learned over its tourist-streaming years that it's not easy to slam the door on everyone else once you're safe and secure in paradise.

Almost half of the two islands' total acreage has been placed in three wildlife preserves: the Bailey Tract on Tarpon Bay Road, the Sanibel-Captiva Conservation Foundation and the J.N. "Ding" Darling Wildlife Refuge. In them you'll find thousands of acres for hiking along nature trails and watching for alligators and turtles below the waters and the many birds above. The islands are permanent home to 40 species of birds and close to 60 species of winter visitors, the first of the snow birds to make Florida their seasonal home. It's all sacred land to the people of Sanibel-Captiva. They have their own vegetation committee, which can issue citations for not watering newly planted trees, or fine an errant driver or builder for destroying or seriously damaging trees or bushes.

With a few modifications, what the Federal Writers Project of the Works Progress

The islands are permanent home to 40 species of birds and close to 60 species of winter visitors.

Every tide and storm washes thousands of specimens of shells onto Sanibel's beaches.

Administration wrote about Sanibel in their wonderful 1939 *Florida: A Guide to the Southernmost State* still applies today:

The island, two miles wide and approximately 12 miles long, is a State game preserve; native and migratory birds are plentiful and can be studied at close range; wild flowers grow profusely in spring and summer; the Gulf and bay offer excellent fishing at all seasons. ... Sanibel Island is notable for the number and variety of seashells on its beaches. Every tide and storm wash(es) ashore thousands of specimens of some 300 varieties.

ACCOMMODATIONS

CONDOMINIUM AND COTTAGE RENTALS

There are many apartment, chalet and cottage
rentals, some by the day, many for a one-week
minimum. Several organizations on the
islands handle such accommodations, including *Captiva Island Realty*, 14970 Captiva
Drive, P.O. Box 189, Captiva 33924, (813)
472-3158; *Sanibel Resort Group*, 1245
Periwinkle Way, Sanibel 33957, (813) 472-
1833 or (813) 472-1001; *The Vacation
Shoppe*, 11595 Kelly Road, Suite 221, Fort
Myers 33908, (813) 454-1400; *Vacation
Properties Network*, 1630 Periwinkle Way,
Sanibel 33957, (813) 472-6565; and *Gulf
Coast Vacations*, 1020 Periwinkle Way, Sanibel
33957, (813) 472-5141 or toll-free:
1-800-633-0042. The largest is:

Priscilla Murphy Realty, Inc.
1177 Causeway Road
P.O. Box 5
Sanibel 33957
Condos-villas-homes/moderate to expensive
Rentals: (813) 472-4883
Rentals, toll-free: 1-800-237-6008
Sales, toll-free: 1-800-233-8829

COTTAGES

MODERATE

*1234 North
Buttonwood
Lane
Sanibel 33957
(813) 472-2609*

BUTTONWOOD COTTAGES

There are not too many accommodations at the point of the promontory near the Sanibel lighthouse, fishing pier and beaches, so we have included these tucked-away retreats, vintage Sanibel cottages, with a pair of twin-bedded efficiencies and a single one-bedroom apartment with queen-size sofa bed. The standards of maintenance are high, and when you come from your beaching and body-bronzing, you'll be able to enjoy all the conveniences of air conditioning, screened porch, cable TV, private bath and fully equipped kitchen, plus laundry facilities on the premises. Another plus is the off-street parking.

APARTMENTS

MODERATE TO
EXPENSIVE

*2669 West Gulf
Drive
P.O. Box 158
Sanibel 33957
(813) 472-1166*

CARIBE BEACH RESORT

There's a heated swimming pool, shuffleboard and volleyball courts along with horseshoes, barbecue grills and bicycles, but this is hardly a resort in the major sense of the word. It's more a modern motel with all the facilities, a two-story cluster of 26 apartments, 23 of them efficiencies, each with a fully equipped kitchen, double Murphy bed and a double pullout couch, plus private deck or balcony and such necessities as private bath, telephone and television. The one-bedroom apartment has a queen-size bed with a pullout couch. There are two cottages: the one-bedroom Outrigger smack on the beach with a queen-

size bedroom in the loft and pullout down-
stairs; and the two-bedroom Spinnaker with a
queen-size bed in one room and twin beds
in the other, along with a pullout couch in
the living room and a bath complete with
whirlpool. Clearly the top of the line.

CASA YBEL RESORT

RESORT

EXPENSIVE

After the Mariner Properties team of planners,
engineers, architects and builders completed
their separate little city of South Seas
Plantation, and a few other premier projects
such as Periwinkle Place (see page 66), they
concentrated on bringing back the
memory of the island's first resort, Casa Ybel
(Cass-a-E-bell). On the sites of the century-
old Sisters Inn and Thistle Lodge, they
transformed 23 acres, about 8 percent the size
of South Seas, into a rambling stretch
of three-story cottages and lodges. They house
114 one- and two-bedroom, two-level suites,
furnished in modern oak and wicker tropical
chic with fully stocked kitchens, king, queen,
double and sofa beds, and all the conveniences.
Each unit has its own private screened porch.

2255 West Gulf Drive
P.O. Box 167
Sanibel 33957
(813) 481-3636
Toll-free: 1-800-237-8906

On campus are a half-dozen tennis courts,
swimming pools for the older and younger
sets, a whirlpool, shuffleboard and volleyball
courts, horseshoes, and a well-stocked fishing
pond for the junior Izaak Waltons in the
group — and Casa Ybel attracts a lot of them.
Those who are enrolled in the nonstop Tiny

Tots program for preschoolers, have fun with toy boat racing, face painting, storytelling and puppet-making. Preteens have Casa Camp with swimming, fishing and tennis lessons, hiking and biking. When camp is not in session, kids can do arts and crafts — make candles, kites, masks and things all their own from shells they collect on the beach. And when they finish all that activity they can rejoin their parents for a bit of rest or recreation elsewhere on the island, returning to rally for meals at one of the best restaurants on the southwest coast of Florida, Truffles at Thistle Lodge, a reconstruction of the old Victorian resort and good enough to deserve its own write-up (see page 51).

COTTAGES

MODERATE TO EXPENSIVE

6460 Sanibel-Captiva Road at Blind Pass
Sanibel 33957
(813) 472-1252
Marina: (813) 472-1112

THE CASTAWAYS

Here's the perfect place for families or couples to establish an island base camp, bedding down in housekeeping bayside or beachfront cottages with fully equipped kitchens, screened porches, cable TV, air conditioning, weekly maid and daily towel service, a laundromat, outdoor barbecue grills, chaise lounges for sunning and a solar-heated swimming pool. There's a fishing pier and full-service marina (open from 7 a.m. to 6 p.m.) where you can purchase everything needed for fishing along with beach umbrellas, rods and reels, canoes and power boats. Four- and eight-hour rentals are available, and you can sign up a guide. The cottage units have one, two and three bedrooms, and there are also efficiency and micro-efficiency accommodations with compact kitchen areas, some with screened porches.

GALLERY MOTEL

MOTEL

MODERATE TO
EXPENSIVE

*541 East Gulf
Drive
Sanibel 33957
(813) 472-1400*

Jack and Betty Reed are the innkeepers of this immaculately maintained cluster of apartments, motel-style rooms, efficiencies and cottages — a total of 31 units — directly on the Gulf beach. Porches and balconies have grand views, and there's a palm-framed swimming pool in center court. Captain Betty is a knowledgeable Coast Guard-licensed guide eager to take guests out on her *Piece A Cake* to do a bit of shelling or sightseeing while munching and lunching on board. You can make the necessary arrangements at the motel office, or call Betty in advance at (813) 472-4575. That's quite a plus in these parts when planning precisely where you want to stay.

COTTAGES
MODERATE

P.O. Box 191
15107 Captiva
Drive
Captiva, 33924
(813) 472-5800

JENSEN'S TWIN PALMS RESORT & MARINA

Located at the marina are wonderful cottages, from one-room to two-bedroom, two-bath units; a laid-back, easy-living way to vacation, with boat rentals and slips to park your own (see page 95).

MOTEL
INEXPENSIVE TO MODERATE

1539 Periwinkle Way
Sanibel 33957
(813) 472-1001

KONA KAI MOTEL

Standard modern motel with one- and two-bedroom efficiencies in a quiet garden setting with a swimming pool and all the conveniences, including three non-smoking rooms. Nothing fancy, not even the rates.

HOTEL
EXPENSIVE

1231 Middle
Gulf Drive
Sanibel 33957
(813) 472-4123
Toll-free:
1-800-443-0909

RAMADA INN ON THE BEACH

A fairly standard link in the nationwide chain but with the added advantage of being on the beach. The 98 rooms are furnished in modern tropical tones with all the amenities, and there's a restaurant/lounge on the premises, along with a heated swimming pool and snack bar, two tennis courts, volleyball court, table tennis and horseshoe facilities as well as rental bicycles.

SANIBEL HARBOUR RESORT & SPA

RESORT

EXPENSIVE

17260 Harbour Pointe Drive
Fort Myers 33908
(813) 466-2166
Toll-free: 1-800-767-7777

This 80-acre resort is not on the islands, but it's as close as such a full-scale facility can be, only a few hundred feet from the tollbooth on the causeway leading to Sanibel. It's on the tip of Punta Rassa, named by the Spanish, and across from Sanibel and Pine islands in San Carlos Bay. Punta Rassa was an important turn-of-the-century shipping port for cattle, rounded up in the wild and driven down the peninsula by a hardy band of cowboys — their lifestyle is portrayed at the living history Cow Camp in the Kissimmee State Park northeast of Lake Wales. The cattle were sold in Cuba and, with a regular communications channel from the island to the mainland, Punta Rassa was where the U.S. first heard of the sinking of the battleship Maine in Havana harbor. Punta Rassa was the site of a popular winter resort, catering to the rich, well-born and famous. The present complex dwarfs its ancestor with an 18-slip marina complete with charter boats for fishing and cruising, a fully staffed tennis center sporting a 5,500-seat stadium, 13 lighted clay and composition courts, and professional instruction including videotaping of all your worst shots. The resort also features an 82-foot free-form swimming pool, a beach on the bayside, a fitness trail, racquetball courts and a 40,000-square-foot spa and fitness center with complete programs to trim the waist and raise the spirits — herbal wraps and loofa scrubs included. The

spa routine continues in the dining room
where the executive chef, working closely with
a registered dietitian, has developed a menu
that offers considerable variety as well as low
calorie-fat-sodium-cholesterol counts. They
are also involved in the "Healthy Cooking
in the '90s" series of seminars held monthly
from October through April, co-sponsored by
the Center for Weight Management at
Southwest Florida Regional Medical Center
in Fort Myers.

Only 20 percent of the resort guests sign
up for the full-scale spa treatments, but many
of the others order from the light gourmet
specials in the Promenade Cafe, where there's
similar weight watching; e.g. an order of
steamed pompano and shrimp accompanied
by a warm orange-sorrel relish costs 215
calories and six grams of fat, and grilled lamb
chops with mixed baby greens in a lemon-
virgin olive oil vinaigrette cost 360 calories
and six grams of fat. We like to start our day
in the Cafe with a spa sampler, a health-giving
smoothie made with bananas, strawberries,
pineapple juice and papaya nectar lightened
with orange blossom water, followed with
an egg-whites-only mushroom omelet, or
maybe go whole hog with poached eggs on
an English muffin or a stack of wheat waffles.
For dinner, if I forgo the spa stuff, I order
the Sanibel snapper with crabmeat in a lemon
beurre blanc, the blackened tuna or the

Southwest crab cake with a spicy cilantro-
freckled cream sauce.

For headier fare there's the showcase Chez
Le Bear Room. Expensive yes, but there I
can start with an interesting risotto made with
Alaskan crab and Florida gator plus prosciutto,
mushrooms and a shower of herbs, or aspara-
gus custard with poached oysters, followed by
rack of lamb flavored with fresh basil and
rosemary and served with zucchini in puff
pastry, or the roast breast of Muscovy duck
served with a date-fig puree and saffron-
enhanced turnips.

After such over- or under-indulgence, I can
tally the calories in the privacy of my room,
one of the 240 handsomely stacked in the
tower. Most of the rooms overlook the bay
and the islands. Sitting on the balcony, drink
in hand, is not a very shabby way to participate in the nightly sunset ritual. There are 24
suites, complete with fully furnished kitchens
(a great place to hide the cookies from your
spa instructor) and a concierge floor with its
own lobby, done in the Victorian manner
with flower-patterned fabrics and lots of
washed-pine pieces. There are more memories
of the Victorian era in the high-ceilinged
lobby with its magnificent twin staircases,
chandeliers that look like gaslights, a giant
hooked rug patterned with seahorses and
shells, and a splendid octagonal pavilion with
a cupola modeled after the one that used to

grace the third floor roof of the old inn. Double deck wraparound porches are great for island and bay-watching, inside or outside, depending on the weather. This resort has it all.

COTTAGES

MODERATE

1223 Buttonwood Lane Sanibel 33957 (813) 472-4262

SEAHORSE COTTAGES

Located at the "other end" of Sanibel, away from the giant resorts and condominiums, near all the history of the old lighthouse where the pace seems slower, the beachgoers less competitive, and the sense of place comforting. Cottage-keeper Susan Rosica provides accommodations compatible with the surroundings, furnishing her one two-bedroom cottage and two one-bedroom units with antiques and her personal touch — which used to include white lace curtains, but they've been replaced with more practical shades. Outside is a private sun deck over-looking a secluded swimming pool filled with fresh water — the salt water is only 200 feet away in San Carlos Bay; and a block away is the Gulf. There are also fully equipped kitchens, private baths, laundry facilities and full temperature control as well as some important extras outside — shower, barbecue grill, fish- and shell-cleaning table.

SONG OF THE SEA

INN

EXPENSIVE

The million dollars spent in 1991 to revive
and refurbish this 1969 pink and green
stucco-and-tile spread of 30 accommodations
was a striking improvement: tile floors, French
Country furnishings, island art, gaily patterned draperies and pillows, full kitchens
with microwaves and all the modern conveniences, plus ceiling fans and screened terraces
and balconies. Management — this is a
Mariner Property owned by the same folks
who brought us South Seas Plantation and
Casa Ybel — is determined to make this "a
European-style seaside inn." Studios and
suites are named for such dream vacation destinations as Amalfi and Portofino; wine and
flowers greet guests upon arrival; and there are
complimentary continental breakfasts, a
library of best sellers, free bicycles, gas barbecue grills, a shuffleboard court, coin-operated
laundry facilities, complimentary tennis at the
Dunes Golf course and a heated swimming
pool with whirlpool. They have also worked
out all kinds of package promotions, including those built around golf, nature pursuits
(you get sun visors and wildlife T-shirts with
that package), fitness and just plain old
romance, built around a two-hour sail and
one-hour massage, catered dinner for two and
an innkeeper, Patricia Slater, who can perform
the wedding ceremony or renewal of vows.
She's no novice, having married almost 900

*836 East Gulf
Drive*
Sanibel 33957
(813) 472-2220
*Toll-free: 1-800-
231-1045*

couples. The fee for such services is donated
to P.A.W.S., a nonprofit organization on the
islands funding costs of spaying, neutering
and caring for abused and homeless cats.

RESORT

EXPENSIVE

P.O. Box 194
Captiva 33924
(813) 472-5111
Toll-free in
Florida: 1-800-
282-3402
Toll-free outside
Florida: 1-800-
237-3102

SOUTH SEAS PLANTATION

My first visit to the northern tip of Captiva
Island was in the early 1970s, just about
the time a spirited, visionary group of
developers — make that dreamers — arrived
on the scene with the cash and courage to
work a major transformation of one of the
top-prize properties in the state. We stayed in
a simple little room that had seen better days,
ate in a thoroughly charming restaurant
named King's Crown (a converted commis-
sary and plantation warehouse), and for a
weekend listened to all the prophets of doom
while we fought off the mosquitoes and
tracked down the history.

Legend has it that 18th century pirates
used the many coves and tucked-away bays to
bury their treasure and keep their women cap-
tive — thus the name Captiva. But those tales
were probably invented by tourist promoters
who wanted to make the islands attractive to
modern-day sailors. The thought of finding
buried doubloons and jewels was not what
brought the first real settler to the tip of land
pointing its finger north. Clarence Chadwick,
inventor of the money-making (literally and
not-so-literally) check writer machine, wanted

to stop the world and get off so he bought the pirates' lairs, all of Captiva and the northern reaches of Sanibel. Importing mainland labor and housing them in cottages in his newly acquired acreage, he planted coconut palms and Key lime trees, many of which still survive, which add their historic presence to the general lushness, the tropical jungle feeling of the resort despite all the buildings, corporate meeting rooms, convention center and all the modern conveniences strategically located but not really overwhelming the place.

Chadwick's plantation prospered, and he built an imposing manor house and other outbuildings. His pioneering achievements are honored in name and giant mural photos in the restaurant called Chadwick's, just outside the main entrance to the complex.

Remembering the history is important as you luxuriate in the certain knowledge that you're in one of the best resorts in the country, a great place for families. Trackless trolleys amble along the resort's only main road, taking guests to and from the multitude of activities and attractions, which include children's programs. These extremely well-organized programs — starting with the 3- to 5-year olds and running to teenagers — include all kinds of arts and crafts, hiking and biking, games and races, and water sports including instructions in waterskiing, sailing, canoeing and windsurfing. Of course, there's a video game center. There's an excellent offshore sailing school where hands-on lessons are given for 27-foot Olympic class sailboats, and the marina has a fleet of boats which management likes to call "The World's Largest Boat Rental Company," everything from 16-foot Wellcrafts to 25-foot Aquasport Cabin Cruisers, great for cruising, diving and fishing.

What about swimming? The resort boasts 18 swimming pools, three outdoor hot tubs and two-and-a-half miles of white sand beach.

Tennis anyone? The Plantation has 22 Laykold courts, scattered throughout the campus so they're convenient to any accommodation chosen; seven are lighted for night play for those who have trouble sleeping, although how that's possible is a bit of a puzzle. There's so much to do all day long — without ever leaving camp — you're usually exhausted at the end of the day, ready to retreat to any one of the 600 handsomely furnished, fussily maintained accommodations from a variety of villas and cottages to four-bedroom homes and the lap of luxury at Land's End Village, the most exclusive of enclaves at the tip of the tip with dramatic panoramas of the Gulf and golf course.

That's right, golf course. A nine-hole par 36, 3,300-yard course with pro shop, rental carts and a resident pro, an active counterpart to the pro who runs the resort's tennis center.

As for nourishment, not to worry. No one in the family will go hungry. Other than the oversized hotel rooms — all with balconies — in Harbourside Village, all accommodations have fully furnished kitchens for those who want breakfast in bed and snack food throughout the day. And if you don't want to dirty the dishes, you can always call room service — they are open for business 7 a.m. to 10 p.m. daily. Then there's the old King's Crown Restaurant with its ambitious continental menu and formal service, and Chadwick's restaurant, open for three meals a day and featuring an eye-popping Sunday champagne brunch (see page 35), Hawaiian luaus and Friday night seafood buffets. The pub alongside the docks has casual food in a casual setting and Mama Rosa's Pizzeria and Uncle Bob's Old Fashioned Ice Cream Shoppe fill in the gaps.

This resort within a resort on its own island has it all, including the record for the world's largest Key lime pie. The pie, a thousand times larger than a normal one, all 250 pounds of it, was made with 16 gallons of Key lime juice, 50 pounds of butter, 117 gallons of condensed milk and 140 pounds of graham cracker crust. The pie tin was assembled from six 4-by-10 sheets of mill finish aluminum. It was quite a fitting tribute to mark the 15th anniversary of South Seas Plantation in 1987.

RESORT

EXPENSIVE

*1451 Middle
Gulf Drive
Sanibel 33957
(813) 472-4151
Toll-free: 1-800-
237-4184*

SUNDIAL BEACH & TENNIS RESORT

Sundial Smiles is the name given by this resort's hip management for its delightfully diversified recreation program, one that keeps families — and families are emphasized here — occupied from dawn to after dusk. For starters, consider adult and junior tennis clinics on a dozen tennis courts, six Laykold and six Har-Tru, tone and trim aerobics, beach walks with knowledgeable guides, water volleyball, bicycle expeditions, shell-a-brations collecting and creating works of art and souvenirs, discovery programs learning about manatees and other dwellers of the deep, cocktail-coketail mixers and parties with the kids doing their own cooking, followed by teen beach bashes with music around the campfire and glow-in-the-dark volleyball.

The programs vary in and out of season, but guests will never be bored, even if it's only swimming or sitting around one of the five pools, including one that's junior Olympic sized. There's also a 10-person jacuzzi, shuffleboard and volleyball courts, water sports with canoes and kayaks available, ping pong and video games. And guests are never far from food — good food — at any point of the sundial. They even offer Japanese fare, and that's unique enough in these parts to deserve a separate write-up (see page 46). The Sundial's Windows on the Green signature room,

which lives up to its name with spectacular
views of the sunsets, is also special enough to
have its own space in the listing of restaurants
(see page 52). For less elaborate sustenance,
there's the poolside bar; snack stuff and deli
fixins' for do-it-yourself meals in The Shoppe,
which also stocks newspapers and magazines,
beach clothes and various toiletries.

There are fully equipped kitchens in each
of the 260 one- and two-bedroom accommodations, each with living room and dining
area, most with a private balcony, patio or
screened porch — you can choose a garden or
Gulf view — and all furnished in a wicker
and tile tropical mode, giving guests the feeling of being on some island in the Caribbean.
There's a variety of package savings at different times of the year and special rates for large
groups taking advantage of the superior
arrangements for corporate meetings.
Management likes to point out that the
Sundial is the only full-service meeting facility
on Sanibel.

RESORT

MODERATE TO
EXPENSIVE

*15951 Captiva
Road
P.O. Box 249
Captiva 33924
(813) 472-5161
Toll-free in
Florida: 1-800-
282-7560
Toll-free outside
Florida: 1-800-
223-5865*

'TWEEN WATERS INN

The waters of the 'Tween are Pine Island
Sound and the Gulf of Mexico, which flank
the 13 acres of buildings new and old, with
accommodations to suit most budgets, most
families, most romantics and beachcombing
loners. The origins go back to a simple little
cabin in the 1920s, cloned into cottages
appealing enough to attract Charles and Anne
Morrow Lindbergh, grateful for the isolation
of the island that allowed them to escape the
incessant pursuit of the press. Another notable
'Tweenie — as they are now known to modern management — was famed cartoonist
J. N. "Ding" Darling, who captured the
shellers with good spirit and his typical sense
of fun, caricaturing them in the familiar
stance of the Sanibel Stoop. His drawings are
preserved with reverence in the inn today,
which also displays and has for sale the works
of a good many other artists portraying contemporary stoopers.

Lindbergh and Darling were early environ-
mentalists. The Lindbergh Foundation with
its myriad projects promoting ecological caus-
es, and the wonderful wildlife refuge named
for Darling, testify to that pioneering involve-
ment. Of course they stayed at 'Tween Waters
Inn. Of course we did the same when we first
voyaged over to this island seeking our own
escape. The look then was far more rugged
than today, with a laid-back concern for
maintenance, with porch screens in need of

repair and the residual reminders of Darling and Great Depression days very much in evidence. There was talk of bulldozing the entire campus — oh, those farseeing developers — and replacing the history with high-rise condominiums. We're glad that cooler, wiser heads prevailed. The inn was saved, and so were all the good memories. The newer, modern 'Tween has the kind of conveniences unheard of in Darling or Lindbergh's philosophy.

Now there's so much more than shells, sand and the setting sun. There's a large heated freshwater swimming pool complete with wading pool and palm frond-covered chickees, poolside bar and grill aptly christened the Oasis. Other attractions include a trio of lighted tennis courts, bocce and shuffleboard courts, plus a fully equipped marina with bait and tackle shop, rental boats, and access to guides for fishing or shelling expeditions. There's also a gift shop and the Pelican's Roost Sportswear Store. Beachfront furnishings include surfing and sailing gear, cabanas, lounges and umbrellas. There are also bicycles for rent for those who want to take landlocked excursions and get in some exercise between sessions at the inn's several eating enclaves.

For snack stuff there's The Crow's Nest, our favorite bar on the island, with live entertainment and offerings of seafood, pasta and grilled chicken Caesar salads, fishwiches layered with fresh grouper or some other catch of the day, steaks and ribs, chicken parmesan, peel-and-eat shrimp garnished with fresh fruit, and Rochester Wings, imported, the menu assures us, via Buffalo.

The Captiva Canoe Club, with an inviting deck strategically placed to watch all the action in the marina, is the place for midday burgers and pizza. The Old Captiva House with its piano lounge and table-groaning Sunday brunches, is the place for serious eating at the inn, as is tastefully described in the listing of restaurants (see page 48).

You can watch the glorious sunsets while working through the excellent menu, or retire to your own digs and the privacy of balcony, porch or patio. Snugly tuck yourself into one of the deluxe or standard rooms, apartments or efficiencies with queen- and king-size beds, fully equipped kitchens, converta-sofas and daily maid service. There are also 52 housekeeping cottages, which can accommodate one to four guests. Most of the cottages have fully equipped kitchens and daily towel service. Weekly maid service is also available for those who want to set up camp for more than a few days.

Some of the rentals include a full American breakfast in the Old Captiva House, and there are modified American plans, including breakfast and dinner, for those staying three or more days. If a Sunday is part of the stay, the Old Captiva House Sunday brunch is included. There are also various package deals and summer reduced rates, some of which are

available during the annual Oktoberfest cele-
brations the last week in the month, and the
inn-sponsored fishing tournaments. The likes
of Curt Gowdy and that ubiquitous walking
commercial, Willard Scott, along with various
sports-celebs, stay at the inn while pursuing
the big ones.

WEST WIND INN

This Gulf front property was our most recent
discovery on the islands and a wonderful one
it was, especially when on our first morning
in residence we wandered into the restaurant
on premises — open only for breakfast and
lunch and only for inn guests. It was terrific,
in concept and execution, service and food.
From the fresh-squeezed OJ to the buttermilk
biscuits and blueberry muffins, pecan and
banana pancakes, French toast filled with
cream cheese and the Lighthouse omelet, "A
Breakfast Beacon" filled with mushrooms,
provolone and spinach. All of it savored in a
room that honors the memory of the
Normandie and the other great ocean liners.
You can learn all about the floating art deco
palace with its galley crew of 14 chefs, 50
assistant cooks, a dozen pastry and ice makers
and 65 helpers. There are great posters and a
fine sense of being in one of the mighty ships
of the 1930s.

Leave the *Normandie* nugget of nostalgia
and charge into the waters of the Gulf and

INN
EXPENSIVE

*3345 West Gulf
Drive*
Sanibel 33957
(813) 472-1541
*Toll-free in
Florida: 1-800-
282-2831*
*Toll-free outside
Florida: 1-800-
824-0476*

all those shells. Walk along the beach, grab a
croquet mallet or a racquet for tennis on one
of their two courts. You can also play shuffleboard or volleyball or rent a bike for touring
around the islands. And after all that, sit
around the palm-framed swimming pool before
retiring to your room for a spell on the
screened balcony or terrace while you get
ready for the nightly sunset ritual. We like
the safes and refrigerators in all the rooms,
the fish- and shell-cleaning hut and the coin
laundry for guests' use. And we like the
attitude of the staff and the management's
special eco-package, which provides special
room rates and savings on bike and boat
rentals, island guides, refuges and books on
the environment. They make a donation for
each reservation to Sanibel's CROW, the Care
and Rehabilitation of Wildlife organization.

DINING

Restaurants

BANGKOK HOUSE

When you're overcome by the urge to indulge
in some grill-it-yourself satay with palate-
awakening peanut sauce, a plate of pla prig,
green, red or yellow curries gentled by
coconut milk, or anything with lemon grass,
head for this little temple of Thai traditional
cuisine. You can adjust the degree of heat to
mild, medium or hot or you can go native,
and set a four-alarm fire in your mouth. Then
reach for a case of Bangkok's Singha beer to
extinguish the flames.

THAI
MODERATE

*1547 Periwinkle
Way, Sanibel
(813) 472-4622
Dinner daily*

BELLINI'S OF CAPTIVA

In loyalty to the Bellini name, you should
start an evening here inside the casually handsome dining room or out on the patio
drinking a peach Bellini cocktail, that cafe
society rage a few seasons back. And while
paying homage to that promotion, study the
menu to decide which of the Northern Italian

ITALIAN
EXPENSIVE

*11521 Andy
Rosse Lane,
Captiva
(813) 472-6866
Dinner daily*

specialties you want to make your evening's entertainment — roast duck with a black currant-cassis sauce, veal scaloppine with mushrooms and brandy-spiked cream sauce, grilled Gulf snapper with a basil-enhanced citrus sauce or the penne Captiva, featuring vodka-zapped mascarpone and smoked salmon.

AMERICAN

EXPENSIVE

15001 Captiva Drive, Captiva
(813) 472-5558
Lunch and dinner daily
No reservations accepted

THE BUBBLE ROOM

Follow the yellow brick road to this monument of nostalgia. Literally. The yellow bricks lead directly to one of the most fascinating collections of stuff found in any restaurant in the nation — and it's all real stuff, not something from the catalogs of kitsch. Why the name? It's taken from those Christmas lights popular a few decades ago, the kind with water bubbling up glass spires. You might recognize other Christmas mementos: the life-like carolers, trolls and tricksters, an explosion of pins, buttons, toys and metal signs. There are more memories immortalized on the menu — Prime Ribs Weismuller, the Eddie Fisherman, Buster Crab Bites, Puttin' On The Ritz and Moon Over Miami. Translation: Tarzan and Jane cuts of beef; grouper poached in parchment; fried crab balls; roast beef, bacon and onion sandwiches with horseradish sauce; and seafood gumbo. The portions are humongous and the desserts outrageous — all 16 of them.

BUD'S ANY-FISH-YOU-WISH

This restaurant's one-of-a-kind name is matched by its unique decor — a handmade ode to informality — and the uniqueness of putting a reliable seafood restaurant, bakery and ice creamery under one roof. They feature such breakfast beauties as Pelican Stuffer, Net-Puller's omelet and Sanibelly Buster, all of them served with freshly baked bread for the "Dingaling Darling's Wake Up Call of the Wild" from 8 a.m. to 11 a.m. Then comes the fresh-squeezed lemonade, limeade and orangeade, the bountifully lively seafood gumbo, the Un'can'ny tuna salad (that's right, out of the sea, not the can), the Hamburger Hamburger (a double), skyscraper clubs and the "fish wish wich" grilled, blackened or fried — we like the grouper and dolphin. Served on their marvelous bread and with some of the best fries in Florida. Dinner means more of the same plus a seemingly infinite variety of Any-Wish-Way fish selections, plus shrimp, steamers, crab and Cajun crawdaddies. And all of it climaxed by indulgence in one of the humongous desserts on display as you enter.

SEAFOOD

INEXPENSIVE TO MODERATE

1473 Periwinkle Way, Sanibel
(813) 472-5700
Breakfast, lunch and dinner daily

AMERICAN

INEXPENSIVE

*Olde Sanibel
Center*
*630 Tarpon Bay
Road, Sanibel*
(813) 472-6622
*Breakfast, lunch
and dinner daily*
*Breakfast only
Sunday*

CALAMITY JANE'S

A fun, informal place to take the family, who will have plenty to look at while working through honestly, well-prepared meals all day long, from breakfast eggs and prime rib(!), Denver and ranchero scrambles and cinnamon-raisin French toast, to super soups and chowders, excellent burgers and sandwiches. The ceiling is plastered with thousands of postcards and there's all kinds of memorabilia relating to the building's original use as the Sanibel Post Office.

CONTINENTAL

EXPENSIVE

*11509 Andy
Rosse Lane,
Captiva*
(813) 472-9129
*Dinner Tuesday
through
Saturday*
*Breakfast
Tuesday through
Saturday*
Sunday brunch
*Reservations
required for
dinner*

CAPTIVA INN

Unique is an overused word these days, but how else to describe this little gem — 40 seats — where you are contacted by chef-owner Evan Snyderman the day before your reservation and informed in detail about the half-dozen entrees he will be serving the next night? You make your choice and then show up at the appointed hour, 7:30 p.m. prompt, to be ushered into an elegant room where it's all crystal, lace, linens and flowers. Champagne is served and the meal commences with a seafood appetizer and proceeds to whatever you ordered. It's all a fixed-price selection and the tariff includes Evan's fresh-brewed soup, a dinner salad, garlic bread, intermezzo sorbets, fresh vegetables and potato croquettes to accompany the entree, which might be fresh Norwegian salmon prepared in a variety of ways, rack of lamb, locally caught grouper or duckling. Coffee and one of the inn's own desserts are included. Unique, yes!

CHADWICK'S

AMERICAN
MODERATE TO EXPENSIVE

The name of this tropical stunner, located a few feet off campus from the entrance to South Seas Plantation, honors the pioneer family who farmed Captiva, growing coconuts and Key limes in the 1920s. A fine photo mural of the clan decorates the bar, which is a good beginning, a place to study the menu and decide where you want to eat. There are cafe, tropical and library settings, and an overall feeling of a plantation home somewhere in the Caribbean. The Sunday brunch, Tuesday Caribbean buffet, complete with steel drum band, and Friday night seafood buffet are alone worth the trip, and there's always a good raw bar selection of freshly shucked oysters, smoked fish dip, burgers and sandwiches in

South Seas Plantation Entrance, Captiva
(813) 472-5111
Lunch and dinner daily
Sunday brunch

the lounge where there's live entertainment. On the more serious side, we like their black bean soup, fried gator tail with horseradish sauce, Jamaican jerk-seasoned chicken with warm tomato salsa, pan-fried fresh grouper with macadamia nuts and ginger-orange sauce, and the T-bone served with elephant garlic. We also like that center court atrium table with its changed-nightly taste of Captiva entrees and fresh vegetables.

AMERICAN

INEXPENSIVE

2413 Periwinkle Way, Sanibel
(813) 472-6111
Lunch and dinner daily

CHEEBURGER CHEEBURGER

Freshly ground beef formed into five sizes for the sampler, semiserious, serious, delirious and group therapy set, cooked to order and presented on toasted kaiser rolls with extras of fries, mushrooms, bacon and onion rings called Chicago. Why Chicago? Who knows? It's not the corporate headquarters of this mini-chain. It's right here. In li'l ole' Sanibel. How smart can the burger bunch get?

DAIRY QUEEN

AMERICAN

INEXPENSIVE

1048 Periwinkle Way , Sanibel
813 472-1170
Lunch and dinner daily

There are no McWendyKings on the islands, and drive-throughs are outlawed, but McDonalds is struggling for its place in the sun and Cheeburger, Cheeburger (see page 36) is a mini-chain in puberty. How then this fast-feeder? It's arguably the best-looking and best-kept Dairy Queen in the nation, and even if it's not, the setting makes it seem that way. It was built early enough — in 1970 — and most important, it's been in the capable, caring hands of Ron Meyer's family since 1971. They're not exactly run-of-the-mill merchandisers or franchisees.

GRAMMA DOT'S SEASIDE SALOON

AMERICAN

MODERATE TO EXPENSIVE

34 North Yachtsman Drive, Sanibel
(813) 472-8138
Lunch and dinner daily

A water-hugging cottage besieged by boats and staffed by an enthusiastic youth corps serving a small selection of snack stuff, outstanding grouper and oyster sandwiches, variations of the classic Caesar with seafood, dolphin with a good honey-citrus glaze, and a pleasing array of Gramma's homemade cakes and pies. If you want Maine lobster, call in advance to reserve it.

**NOUVELLE
AMERICAN**

EXPENSIVE

*Captiva Village
Square
14970 Captiva
Road, Captiva
(813)472-6006
Dinner daily
October through
April*

THE GREENHOUSE

We run out of superlatives when discussing
the merits of this tiny enclave of casual ele-
gance. Ariel and Danny Mellman are in
charge here. Danny's talents took him all the
way to the James Beard house in New York
where he was a guest chef for one of the 1992
Discovery Dinners. His genius can be
observed in the open kitchen. Nobody on the
islands — or in West Florida and maybe the
entire South — is doing a better clam chowder with its smoked bacon, heavy cream and a
hint of saffron. And nobody in these parts is
having such fun with the likes of cilantro pap-
pardelle and Thai-curried chicken in
coconut-pumpkin seed sauce; pan-seared veni-
son coated with pepper and served on wild
mushroom sauce with pecan-jalapeno flecked
cornbread and a syrup spiked with Jack
Daniel's. We especially like his inspired treat-
ment of sweetbreads, coated with garlic and
tomato-flavored mascarpone, then wrapped in
romaine before grilling and serving on rosemary risotto with chinoise sauce.
And for finishers, check Dan's "Cosmic
Confections," made on the premises of
course, like everything else he serves in this
handsome little house with contemporary
artwork displayed on the walls.

HARBOR HOUSE RESTAURANT

SEAFOOD

MODERATE

1244 Periwinkle Way, Sanibel
(813) 472-1242
Lunch and dinner daily

Since 1981 Anne and Bill Walter have been in charge of this cozy little blue and white low-rise, a homey, family-oriented nautical escape to which they bring a full measure of their devotion — creating excellent chowders, crab-meat-stuffed Florida lobster, fried shrimp, scallops, flounder and oysters, along with broiled grouper and snapper. All that serves as prelude to the Key lime pie with the name-sake ingredient coming from their own trees. They pick the limes daily during the season.

ISABELLA'S

ITALIAN-AMERICAN

INEXPENSIVE

1528 Periwinkle Way, Sanibel
(813) 472-0044
Lunch and dinner Monday through Saturday
Limited menu Sunday afternoons and evenings

Pizza is just one of the Italian-American treats Isabella will deliver to your table or your home. There's also a good selection of the kind of veal and pasta dishes you've learned to expect, but not always respect, from pizzerias of this type — lasagna and gnocchi, ravioli and manicotti.

ITALIAN

INEXPENSIVE

*Island Tower
Plaza*
*1619 Periwinkle
Way, Sanibel*
(813) 472-1581
*Lunch and
dinner daily*
No charge cards

ISLAND PIZZA

Eat in, take out or have it delivered, whether you want a thin or thick crust pizza, calzone, giant sub, chicken wings, corn dogs, lasagna or spaghetti noon or night. Even baby back ribs or grilled chicken Caesar salad. The two-story with cathedral ceiling is a unique woodsy setting for a pizzeria, but after all, this is Sanibel.

AMERICAN

MODERATE TO
EXPENSIVE

*1223 Periwinkle
Way, Sanibel*
(813) 472-1771
Dinner daily

THE JACARANDA

Here's a woodsy tropical retreat that has it all: screened outdoor patio, inside lounge with live entertainment, dancing and high spirits; raw bar, special early bird dinner savings and a great serving staff. It's a good destination for families as well as romantics seeking that perfect rendezvous, and it has a real sense of place. It's Sanibel's original island bar, which back in the 1960s was known as Scotty's Pub. Today it's where we go for marvelous mussels, those glorious green lip giants from New Zealand, along with some other imports — Maine Lobster and Angus beef. Local waters provide the mahi-mahi, tuna, swordfish, grouper and snapper prepared any which way and with a good choice of sauces. A final two pluses: the farinaceous fare and the good wine list.

JEAN-PAUL'S FRENCH CORNER

FRENCH

EXPENSIVE

708 Tarpon Bay Road, Sanibel

(813) 472-1493

Dinner daily October through April

Reservations strongly recommended

Since 1978 this free-standing two-story has been setting the standards for fine French food. But don't judge this book by its unkempt, overgrown looks in the summer when it's closed. Go back in the season and start your dinner with some soft shell crabs provencal, a half-dozen snails or a chilled soup, then try a duckling with some kind of fruit sauce, fresh Norwegian salmon with a fine dill-flecked cream sauce, filet mignon with a green peppercorn coating, a fresh Florida ocean fillet or one of chef Jean-Paul's specials. Conclude with a fine creme caramel or a surprisingly good pecan pie, while you finish the last sips of wine from a select list, saluting the Gallic genius of owner-chef Jean Paul Cavonie.

AMERICAN

INEXPENSIVE TO
MODERATE

6520-C Pine
Avenue, Sanibel
(813) 472-5353
1036 Periwinkle
Way, Sanibel
(813) 472-6939
Lunch and
dinner daily
No credit cards

LAZY FLAMINGO I, II

They could change that Lazy to Industrious.
This flamingo has two nests, the original
one, which the locals prefer, in "Beautiful
Downtown Santiva," and a newer one on
Periwinkle close to the causeway in colors you
can't miss. Pink, pink, pink, next door to
the Dairy-Queen red, red, red. The new one
sports the biggest bar on Sanibel and it's
stocked with the usual, plus five large-screen
TVs fed by satellite dish. Both feature a fine
variety of munchies at pocketbook-pleasing
prices: conch salad, fritters and chowder,
peel-and-eat beer-steamed shrimp, mesquite-
grilled grouper sandwiches and our favorite
fare — burgers and the Caesar salad with
mesquite-grilled chicken breast served with
excellent garlic bread.

CONTINENTAL

INEXPENSIVE TO
MODERATE

Seashore Shops
362 Periwinkle
Way, Sanibel
(813) 472-0303
Breakfast, lunch
and dinner daily

LIGHTHOUSE CAFE

We've made this simple little cafe on the lighthouse side of Sanibel our breakfast
headquarters since the early '70s, getting there
as early as seven or as late as three and order-
ing the extraordinarily good muffins, seafood
fritatas, turkey Benedict, any of their panhan-
dled egg dishes or what they call their
homespun hotcakes, wholewheat honeys with
granola. Luncheon sandwiches are real
mouth-benders. For lunch we like their Philly

cheesesteak sandwich or the seafood griddle and for dinner their blackened dolphin, char-grilled chicken cordon bleu and barbecue ribs. And anytime is good for one of Catherine Billheimer's fabulous desserts, the Key lime pie, blueberry or blackbottom cheesecake. Catherine is married to Michael who, with his brother Kim, make up the highly personable ownership team. The family's history as restaurateurs on the island goes all the way back to pre-causeway days when their aunt, Betty Sears, ran the Case Marina where Gramma Dot's is today. She and her partner, Evelyn Pearson, also ran the Nutmeg House. This cafe is true to the traditions.

McT's SHRIMP HOUSE & TAVERN

SEAFOOD

MODERATE TO EXPENSIVE

1523 Periwinkle Way, Sanibel
(813) 472-3161
Dinner daily

There are endless schools of fish and squadrons of shrimp swimming in and out of this kitchen, which calls them all kinds of cute names: shrimp Oscar de la Renta, Shrimp Marie (named after an Italian pinup barmaid of the late 1800s), bronzed swordfish, Zydeco Tous Pa Tous Shrimp (fried and blackened Cajun style with bleu cheese-ranch dressing), and McT's Catch All, fried or sauteed fish fillet, oysters, scallops and shrimp. Steak, chicken and ribs are also given a place on the menu, but here we eat something from the sea. Start with McT's conch chowder, crab-filled mushroom caps hollandaise or shark fingers ("Did you know they had hands?")

and move on to broiled salmon or Maryland-style crab cakes, the shrimp or scallops stir-fried with fresh veggies. In summer months we feast on their reasonably priced Maine lobster. Anytime of the year we finish with their mud pie or something from their bakery — not far away at Bud's Any Fish You Wish, also owned by McT, otherwise known as Buddy Lo Cicero.

NOUVELLE AMERICAN

EXPENSIVE

6460 Sanibel-Captiva Road, Sanibel
(813) 472-0033
Dinner daily

THE MAD HATTER

There are so many things to like about this restaurant. There's the glorious view of the sunset, the highly professional and pleasant staff, the excellent California wines and the comfortable, completely non-smoking room, with 44 seats, a perfect size for a chef to exercise his talents. Robert Pascuzzi meets the challenge admirably, changing his menu monthly and headlining it with such stunning starters as grilled sea scallops in ginger-coconut cream, and savory salmon Napoleons layered with fried wonton skins, seasoned with capers, horseradish and shallots in a grainy mustard chive vinaigrette. The half-dozen entrees are equally innovative and masterfully produced: grilled tuna with warm ginger miso vinaigrette served with wild mushrooms, wilted greens and a wasabi cream zinger; pan-seared peppercorn-crusted beef tenderloin accompanied by herb-enhanced spaetzle and spaghetti squash. Those are only a few of the boredom-breakers from chef Pascuzzi, who's given full rein by owners Brian and Jayne Baker. They are two more reasons to like this special place. Brian and Jayne were the first staffers hired in 1983 when The Mad Hatter opened. Seven years later they bought the place.

MATT & HARRY'S STEAK HOUSE

AMERICAN

MODERATE TO EXPENSIVE

The same perfectionists in charge of Timbers run the show here — as you'll quickly learn if you order some of their fresh fish of the day, including superior salmon with dill sauce and chargrilled shrimp on a skewer. But the head-liners here are the New York strip sirloins, the T-bones, prime rib, lamb, pork and veal chops. Occupying the space where Timbers used to be, it's the place on the islands for the best beef.

975 Rabbit Road, Sanibel
(813) 472-8666
Dinner daily Mid-November through May

CONTINENTAL

MODERATE TO
EXPENSIVE

*11546 Andy
Rosse Lane,
Captiva*
(813) 472-3434
*Lunch and
dinner daily*
No credit cards

THE MUCKY DUCK

The only mucky duck on the menu is the luncheon Mucky Duck Super Frankfurter. You can get some Ducky fried chicken and for dinner, roast duckling a l'orange. But, in this beachfront pub that provides a casual, comfortable arena for the nightly sunset-watching ritual, we prefer their superb barbecued bacon-wrapped shrimp, broiled dolphin with a dill-flecked cream sauce or good old-fashioned English fish 'n' chips. Start with a cup of clam chowder — the white, New England kind — and finish with a homemade chocolate walnut brownie.

AMERICAN

EXPENSIVE

*Sundial Beach &
Tennis Resort*
*1451 Middle
Gulf Drive,
Sanibel*
(813) 472-4151
*Dinner Tuesday
through
Saturday*
*Reservations
required*

NOOPIE'S

Tourists yearning for the Japanese steak house approach to fine dining should head here. Tucked into the premier resort of Sanibel, it's where you sip your Sapporo or sake — or maybe a Samurai martini or sakatini with OJ — while watching the blade-brandishing chefs go through their paces deftly slicing the shrimp and sea scallops, chicken breasts, lobster tails, sirloins and filet mignons, serving them proudly to the enraptured guests seated around the teppenyaki table. You start with some sushi, then spoon into thin broth and crunch a cooling salad while the swordsman cuts and grills before your eyes, and your tablemates find it impossible to resist discussing their Japanese cars, TVs, Walkmen and maybe the trade balance.

THE NUTMEG HOUSE

When we first started visiting these islands this was our favorite restaurant, run by a pair of lovely ladies, Betty Sears and Evelyn Pearson. It's still a favorite, run by David Wackerman, but now he's got a lot of competition for our attention. We still like the garden atmosphere, the classical music and jazz on Tuesday, Wednesday and Sunday and such specialties as oysters Rockefeller, designer pizzas, veal Francaise, steak Diane and the roast duckling with a honey-orange-raspberry sauce. We also like the wine list and the Cruvinet allowing for tastings by the glass.

CONTINENTAL

EXPENSIVE

*Nutmeg Village
2761 West Gulf
Drive, Sanibel
(813) 472-1141
Dinner daily*

CONTINENTAL

EXPENSIVE

'Tween Waters
Inn
Captiva Drive,
Captiva ·
(813) 472-5161
Dinner daily
and Sunday
brunch

OLD CAPTIVA HOUSE

A carefully preserved leftover from the good
old days with weathered woods and breezy
patio-porch, it is the place where we start our
meals with some of their special Captiva
bisque, a rich and creamy coming together of
shrimp and fresh herbs spiked with brandy.
From there we move on to the fresh scallops
sauteed with prosciutto and capers, presented
on a bed of pinkish tomato angel hair pasta
with a tomato-basil beurre blanc, roasted pork
tenderloin Chasseur, saltimbocca prepared the
classic way with olive oil, prosciutto, sage,
lemon and white wine, or the equally classic
coq au vin served with a fine cabernet sauce.
The Sunday brunch is sensational.

AMERICAN

EXPENSIVE

Palm Ridge
Plaza
2330 Palm
Ridge Place,
Sanibel
(813) 395-2300
Lunch and
dinner daily
Dinner only
during the
summer

PALM RIDGE CAFE

This is a quiet and cozy little cafe, all pink
and wicker with etched glass palms and a fine
upfront wine bar that is a splendid staging
area during the peak times of the season when
they're open for lunch as well as dinner.
Midday we like the Cobb and Florida fruit
salads and the crab-shrimp melt, and for dinner, the stuffed mushrooms Romanoff,
chargrilled pork chops, veal Florentine or
Oscar, sea scallops sauteed with lemon, butter
and white wine sprinkled with parsley; the
pan blackened marinated swordfish or the

chicken Eduardo which translates to a breast filled with broccoli, mushrooms and Swiss cheese then baked and blessed with basil beurre blanc. Creme brulee is the proper conclusion.

RITZ DINER

AMERICAN
INEXPENSIVE

The 1950s with a vengeance. Neon and chrome. Flip waitresses, a savvy owner who could play the role in a sitcom, kitchen crew on view, and a menu that's as much fun as the surroundings and the staff — meatloaf, salisbury steak, brisket and P.B. & J. sandwiches; calves liver and onions and a bunch of other complete dinners — soup or salad, rolls, vegetables and potato — at bargain prices; shakes and floats, banana splits and sodas.

2407 Periwinkle Way, Sanibel
(813) 472-6882
Breakfast, lunch and dinner daily
No credit cards

SUNSHINE CAFE

NOUVELLE
AMERICAN
MODERATE

A local favorite — despite its postage stamp size and limited menu — this informal interpreter of the California approach to culinary innovation has a few tables out on a narrow wooden porch that has an authentic island feel about it. The menu is shifted regularly and is executed by an on-view kitchen with great finesse and style. Whether we have a salad or one of their sandwiches — which they should patent — we come away pleased.

Captiva Village Square, Captiva
(813) 472-6200
Lunch and dinner daily
No credit cards

SEAFOOD

MODERATE TO
EXPENSIVE

*703 Tarpon Bay
Road, Sanibel*

(813) 472-3128

Dinner daily

THE TIMBERS RESTAURANT &
THE SANIBEL GRILL

One of the island's most popular — and profitable — restaurants moved into this second-floor spread in 1992, putting a grill, raw bar, and overhead TVs on one side and the main dining room on the other. In the Grill there are such headliners as the spinach and three-cheese dip, smoked bluefish Caesar salad and chicken quesadillas wrapped in a tortilla and served with sour cream and a very good salsa. In the main dining room, framed by windows, we like the oysters Florentine, clams and shrimp casino, broiled sea scallops and the house feast, broiled or fried seafood platters. If your palate is landlocked, don't worry, the steaks here are reliable. The Timbers is open every night for dinner; The Sanibel Grill for lunch and dinner (serving until midnight) daily.

AMERICAN

MODERATE

*15183 Captiva
Drive, Captiva*

(813) 472-9444

*Lunch and
dinner daily
except
Wednesday*

TIMMY'S NOOK

Captiva's oldest restaurant clutches a side cove of sand at the big bend in the road leading to South Seas Plantation. This aptly named roadside seafood shack has walls that talk — of the good old days before the bridge and causeway brought the invasion from the mainland, and everything was real easy. From

the city of the Big Easy — New Orleans —
Timmy has brought all the spices of the back
bayous. Here they serve Cajun blackened fish,
shrimp and steak, along with grouper imperial
and seafood Vera Cruz. Saturday is prime rib
night.

TRUFFLES AT CASA YBEL

Opened in 1988 by the cuisine management
whose other restaurants — Chef's Garden,
Bayside, Plum's Cafe, Truffles and Villa
Pescatore — are all the rage in Naples, this
pleasantly served spinoff is a handsomely
designed reconstruction of a Victorian
mansion built by a pioneer family who ran
the island's first inn. The view of Gulf and
gardens is sensational, the kitchen highly
competent. They prepare everything from
giant hot dogs and taco salads to fettuccine
primavera, spiced pork loin, shrimp car-
bonara, vegetable stir-fry and New York
strip steak. The Sunday brunch is a beaut,
and you can start your expedition to this recreation of Sanibel's early history by sipping a
bit at the pool bar.

AMERICAN

**MODERATE TO
EXPENSIVE**

Casa Ybel Resort
*2255 West Gulf
Drive, Sanibel*
(813) 472-9200
*Lunch and
dinner daily*
Sunday brunch

AMERICAN

EXPENSIVE

*Sundial Beach
and Tennis
Resort*

*1451 Middle
Gulf Drive,
Sanibel*

(813) 472-4151

*Breakfast, lunch
and dinner daily*

WINDOWS ON THE GREEN

A sensationally situated room true to its
name, with a great view of surf and shore pro-
viding one of the reasons for dining here.
There are also crab cakes served with a sharp
mustard sauce, the crabmeat-stuffed arti-
chokes bearnaise, sherry-spiked conch
chowder and Louisiana gumbo, the authentic
variety brought to these shores from New
Orleans by the former executive chef Peter
Harman, whose recipes are still being executed by the back room. While he's over on the
mainland, his successors are grilling filet
mignon and serving it with caramelized
onions and sauteed mushrooms; topping red
snapper with blue crab and bearnaise, bronz-
ing shrimp and serving them with a small
tenderloin bordelaise. Pan-seared dolphin and
cedar-planked salmon enhanced by a dill
beurre blanc are two of my favorites. The
expanded Cruvinet allows 16 premium wines
to be served by the glass. A class act.

Delicatessens, Caterers and Takeout

B-HIVE

A class delicatessen with a pretty fair selection of beer and wine, all kinds of cut meats and cheeses and for takeout, more than 90 different subs and sandwiches, including 10 inches of Philly cheese-steak layered with sauteed onions; turkey on rye with cranberries and coleslaw; a Dagwood with everything; and their most notable invention, the Sanibel Seafood Sub with crab, lobster and shrimp, lots of lettuce, onions, tomatoes and hot drawn butter.

2407 Periwinkle Way, Sanibel
(813) 472-1277

CAROLYN'S CUSTOM CATERING

Expert caterers alongside the Reel Eel Seafood Shop, Carolyn's has an extensive takeout menu with all kinds of fresh harvest from the sea prepared any which way but loose in disposable pans, plus made-on-the-premises breads, hors d'oeuvres, and such goodies as fudge praline and raspberry jam bars, fresh berry and Key lime pies.

1723 Periwinkle Way, Sanibel
(813) 472-2674

Periwinkle Place, 2075 Periwinkle Way, #37, Sanibel
(813) 472-3837

CHOCOLATE EXPRESSIONS

My favorite is the chocolate walnut fudge. Other specialties are the hand-dipped items, truffles and molded chocolate everything.

11500 Andy Rosse Lane, Captiva
(813) 472-2374

ISLAND STORE

This one-stop shop has everything from groceries, ice cream bars and Lotto tickets to the Sunday morning paper. The deli section has its own version of the Reuben they call the Beachcomber. Some other specialties are the Old Fashioned, a roast beef and turkey sandwich with Swiss cheese and special sauce, lettuce and tomato; and the Classic Sub with Italian deli meats and dressings. Or you can choose from the many selections seducing you from the display counters and build your own sandwich. Layer the stuff in a croissant for a change of pace and taste.

SHOPPING

Beach and Casual Clothing

BAILEY'S CASUAL WEAR

For women there are Karen Kane and Action
Wear, and for men, Nautica and Jansen.
In the shoe department are the ever-popular
Keds and Ninewear.

Bailey's Shopping Center
2477 Periwinkle Way and Tarpon Bay Road, Sanibel
(813) 472-1636

CANDICE ARNOLD'S

Casual and dressy women's clothing by
the area's most popular designers, such as
Laura Lane.

110 Chadwick's Square, Captiva
(813) 472-3777

CHICO'S

You know they're doing something right if
they have four locations in this area — two in
Sanibel and two in Captiva. They outgrew

their store in Chadwick's Square so they built another and kept the small one. This is the place to get upscale casual clothing. Everything is 100 percent cotton prewashed and pre-shrunk. The oversized T-shirts make excellent beach coverups and most of the clothing is unisex — camp shirts and unconstructed blazers. They also have great accessories — belts, jewelry — and a friendly, courteous staff with incredible enthusiasm.

2330 Palm Ridge Road, Sanibel, (813) 472-3773;
Periwinkle Place, Sanibel, (813) 472-0202;
Chadwick's Square, Captiva, (813) 472-4426;
CHICO & LUCKY'S, Chadwick's Square, Captiva,
(813) 472-6101

DUNHAM'S OF MAINE

Down-easters know and honor the name. They've been in business in the cold, cold North since 1887. They sell top-quality, brand-name women's and men's casual and sportswear, as well as women's handbags and smart, understated accessories.

Sanibel Square
2242 Periwinkle Way, Sanibel
(813) 472-3059 or (813) 472-1518

FRANGI-PANI RESORTWEAR NATURALLY

The latest in shorts and tops, T-shirts, accessories and a few suits. They specialize in clothing made of natural fibers in brand names such as Cotton Connection, Back East and New Era.

Chadwick's Square
P.O. Box 425, Captiva
(813) 395-0717

ISLAND BEACH COMPANY

The hottest swimsuits in Captiva can be found in this shop, selling brands such as Too Hot Brazil, Le Blanca and Jantzen. They also have coverups and casual clothing for men and women.

14820 Captiva Drive S.W., P.O. Box 425, Captiva
(813) 472-3272

JOYCE JORDAN

Some of the finest casual clothing for women can be found here, including brand names such as Joan Voss and David Darth.

Periwinkle Place
2075 Periwinkle Way, Sanibel
(813) 472-0505

MAGGIE ELLIOTT

This is just the sort of shop we love to discover. Owner Maggie Elliott immigrated here to escape Wisconsin's winters. She keeps a pot of coffee brewing and a little snack for the sweet tooth to welcome her customers, and her family photos on the walls add a personal touch. The hunter green decor, with its oak and Oriental accents, is charming. You won't find trendy beach or Florida-fun clothing here. Everything is a classic you'll be able to wear to dinner or the office as casual resort wear, all updated for the '90s.

2075 Periwinkle Way, Sanibel
(813) 472-2230

OLDE HOUSE SHOPPE

This is the oldest boutique on the island, located in the heart of Olde Sanibel Shopping center in the historic Cooper house built in 1891. It features clothing from around the world for the woman who wants a soft, romantic look.

Olde Sanibel Shopping Center
630 Tarpon Bay Road, Sanibel
(813) 472-2692

SANIBEL ISLAND PELICAN COMPANY

Home of the popular shelling shoes, shelling
slippers and all kinds of T-shirts.

Ritzy's Islander Center
2407 Periwinkle Way, Sanibel
(813) 472-5953

SILKEN TOUCH

As the name suggests, this shop is filled with
beautiful silk creations from casual to elegant,
and all the colorful accessories to go with
them. They carry such name brands as Adam
Douglass Silk, and Restless Washable Silk,
always in the latest colors and styles.

Tahitian Gardens Shopping Center
1983 Periwinkle Way, Sanibel
(813) 395-0333

SILKS BY LAHJA

Finnish-born Lahja Seppa-Tischler opened
this shop in the '80s to showcase and sell her
beautifully hand-painted silkwear. You can
watch her create while you browse. The silk
stretcher, paints and brushes are set up in the
center of the shop so you can see belts, dress-
es, scarves, shirts and pillows come to life
with bursts of color.

The Village Shops
2340 Periwinkle Way, Sanibel
(813) 472-0003

SPOIL ME

Specializes in women's swimwear and coverups for the discriminating shopper with the hottest name brands — Oscar de la Renta, La Blanca, Too Hot Brazil and Roxanne.

Tahitian Gardens
2017 Periwinkle Way, Sanibel
(813) 472-0999

THE SPORTY SEAHORSE

This is advertised as Sanibel's only department store. They also claim to have the largest selection of swimsuits and T-shirts on the island.

362 Periwinkle Way, Sanibel
(813) 472-1858

T-SHIRT PLACE OF SANIBEL

You can create your own design and pick your colors for a personal mix and match.

Periwinkle Place Shopping Center
2075 Periwinkle Way #13, Sanibel
(813) 472-2392

TAHITIAN SURF SHOP

One of the best places on the island for brand
name — Stussy, Mossimo, Gotcha, Club,
Raisins — swimsuits, surf gear, casuals and all
sorts of accessories for guys and gals.

Tahitian Gardens Shopping Center
2015 Periwinkle Way, Sanibel
(813) 472-3431

TRADER RICK'S

They pride themselves on their exclusive,
out-of-the-ordinary items such as Hawaiian
rayon by Rainbow Jo, cotton-laced items,
hand-painted cottons by designer V.C. Toria
and U.S.A. cotton. The extensive line of
jewelry and the small children's corner are
other reasons to stop in.

1551 Periwinkle Way, P.O. Box 144, Sanibel
(813) 472-4322

WEST WIND SURF SHOP

Stop here for the latest in swimwear, casual
clothing, sweats and T's, and designer sun-
glasses. They feature the newest arrivals from
Ritchie Swimwear, Take Cover, Billabong,
Vision, Side Out Sport and Fresh Produce.

Periwinkle Place Shopping Center
2075 Periwinkle Way, Sanibel
(813) 472-3490

WING'S WILDLIFE BOUTIQUE

Unique wildlife designs from Harlequin are found on clothing here, using the talents of many local artists, including the notable Michael Latona, who bring their views of the islands to life.

1700 Periwinkle Way, Sanibel
(813) 472-2251

Gifts, Jewelry, Shells, Souvenirs

CONGRESS JEWELERS

Check the catalog showing their large selection of fine jewelry in 14- and 18-carat gold from well-known designers. They also carry Judith Lieber handbags.

2075 Periwinkle Way, #35, Sanibel
(813) 472-4177; toll-free: 1-800-882-6624

ENCHANTED MERMAID

This is the perfect shop for collectors. They have Hummels, limited edition wildlife prints, Andrea figurines, gold and silver jewelry and many unique gifts.

Periwinkle Place #43, Sanibel
(813) 472-2686

GIFTS FROM THE SEA

The shop is named for Anne Morrow Lindbergh's book, but is really a Victorian gift shop that carries lace everything, books, aromatherapy products, crystal window hangers, antique jewelry, hand-painted porcelain and a huge selection of greeting cards.

Old Sanibel Center
630 Tarpon Bay Road, Sanibel
(813) 472-8800

HANDWORKS OF SANIBEL

Fine handcrafted products such as quilts, jewelry, hand-painted clothing and other wearable art.

Palm Ridge Place
2330 Palm Ridge Road, Sanibel
(813) 395-0080

ISLAND GIFTS and ISLAND GARAGE

Ohio natives James and Mary Thomas opened this conglomerate gift shop-auto repair center in 1975. The gift shop sells the handcrafts of Mary and her daughter, which are made from the shells of the area and other beaches around the world — beautiful wind chimes, wall plaques, jewelry and shirts. The garage, run by James, is busy with repairs and their 24-hour wrecker service.

1609 Periwinkle Way, Sanibel
(813) 472-4318

THE MOLE HOLE

A portion of the unusual merchandise here represents collections from travels throughout the world. However, most of the items are home-grown. Craftspeople and artists from the good ole U.S. are the main attraction, with exotic wildlife replicas, crystal, lamps, tableware and Oriental pieces.

Periwinkle Gardens
551 Periwinkle Way, Sanibel
(813) 472-2767

NEPTUNE'S TREASURES

Home of the world famous $24\frac{1}{2}$-inch conch shell that was retrieved from 40-foot-deep water 20 miles offshore. Also fascinating are the buffalo bones with arrowheads embedded in them. Most everything here has its own tale. Standing amid fossils, coral-covered bottles, coins and lanterns from shipwrecks, makes my mind wander through time to an era when Native Americans, pirates, and the explorers populated the area. There are also shell collections from all corners of the world. Ed Hanley, who with his wife Jackie, owns this nautical gift shop, is a diving-shelling-fishing guide in Sanibel and writes a column in the local paper on shell collecting.

Tree Tops Centre
1101 Periwinkle Way, #105, Sanibel
(813) 472-3132

OFFSHORE NAUTICAL

Owner Captain Jerry Sidock has 30 years'
experience sailing ships, including some he
built himself. He's been around the world
several times, sailed the seven seas, and
managed to fit in studies of nautical electronics at two major universities in Texas. All this
has helped him create a unique shop filled
with collectibles from all points of the globe.
The shop is also a National Ocean and
Atmospheric Agency and Defense Mapping
Agency, which makes it *the* headquarters
for nautical charts. His library is stocked with
books on sailing, fishing, boating, shelling,
cruising and Florida.

Periwinkle Gardens
1551 Periwinkle Way, Sanibel
(813) 472-2224

PERIWINKLE PLACE

Periwinkle Place is a shopper's delight with 35 shops, including Bananas, The Store With Appeal, Toys Ahoy, Her Sports Closet and The Noisy Oyster. To amuse those with short shopping attention spans, there's Japanese chime music, a center court fountain and playground, and the Snooty Fox restaurant [(813) 472-2525], which is open for lunch and dinner every day . The restaurant has a special menu for the under-12 set, along with good sandwiches, burgers, ravioli and char-broiled chicken, all at moderate prices.

2075 Periwinkle Way, Sanibel

THE PROUD HERON

Gemstones from around the world are purchased by owner Maruchy and put into the hands of designer J.C. Velarde, to create masterpieces in art and fine jewelry. His creations have been sold in shops in Miami Beach, on Fifth Avenue and in Europe. Accessories, objects of art, crystal and jewelry are also purchased from countries around the world — crystal from Sweden, Thai wood and bronze sculptures and Latin American handcrafts.

The Village Shops
2340A, Periwinkle Way, Sanibel
(813) 472-1043

RENE'S ARTISANS OF FINE JEWELRY, INC.

Rene is proud of his one-of-a-kind jewelry.
He loves to create pieces to suit each
customer's personality.

630 Tarpon Bay Road, Suite 9, Sanibel
(813) 472-5544

SANDPIPER OF SANIBEL

A menagerie of beautiful stuffed animals,
accessories for the home and kitchen, wind
chimes, hats, bags, purses, baskets and all
sorts of knickknacks from around the world
can be found in this gift shop. They cover the
walls, floors, even the ceilings. Some items
are made of shells and materials found in the
Sanibel-Captiva area and make wonderful
keepsakes from your vacation on the islands.

2330 Palm Ridge Road, Sanibel
(813) 472-4645

SHOWCASE SHELLS

A shell collector's paradise with many hard-to-
find shells, including some exotic specimens
from around the world.

Island Plaza
1614 Periwinkle Way, Sanibel
(813) 472-1971

A TOUCH OF SANIBEL POTTERY

Most of the pieces are high-fired stoneware in
this studio that produces four-star pottery
in many styles such as salt-glazed from
Minnesota, Jim Rice's elaborately decorated
rococo, pieces by Ken Jensen from Micanopy,
and Steve Jepson from Geneva.

1544 Periwinkle Way, Sanibel
(813) 472-4330

CONVENIENCES

Baby-sitting Services and Baby Supplies

RABBIT ROAD CENTER FOR CHILDREN

"Island Visitors Welcome" reads the sign, and they accept infants through school-age children. The programs are designed to entertain your little ones while you relax in the sun or do whatever else parents like to do when they get some free time.

975 Rabbit Road, Sanibel
(813) 472-8687

SANIBEL RENTAL SERVICE

For those with wee ones, you'll be glad to know there's a shop where you can rent baby conveniences — most of the time necessities — such as swings, front- and back-packs, booster seats, child gates, large and small strollers, playpens, car seats, porta-cribs, full cribs and walkers. They have everything

under the sun to keep a smiling face on you
and the tots. They also have beach loungers,
chairs and umbrellas.

Sanibel Square
2246 Periwinkle Way, Sanibel
(813) 472-5777

Barber and Beauty Shops

PAT'S HAIR KAIR

Body waxing for smooth legs and a perfect
bikini line, manicures, pedicures and facials,
all can be found in this shop, along with the
usual hair-care services.

2248 Periwinkle Way, Sanibel
(813) 472-2425

HAIR, SKIN & NAILS

In this full-service salon they use Matrix hair
and skin care products and offer every service
imaginable to make you look and feel like
a million. Their massage therapy and total
make-over package is a way to rejuvenate
yourself and leave your vacation looking and
feeling like a new person.

Periwinkle Place, 2nd Floor, Sanibel
(813) 395-2220

NEW SPIRIT HAIR DESIGN

If you like setting yourself apart from the crowd, this is the place to go for a hairstyle that is specially designed for you, using Matrix, Sebastian and Nexxus products. Their nail care specialist gives a great manicure.

1715 Periwinkle Way, Sanibel
(813) 472-HAIR; (813) 472-2371

SANIBEL BARBERS

This is a unisex barbershop good for the whole family. Men can get an old-fashioned barber cut or an up-to-date style.

Bailey's Shopping Center
Periwinkle Way and Tarpon Bay Road, Sanibel
(813) 472-5626

SANIBEL BEAUTY SALON

Get a cut-and-curl the way they used to do it or try a new fashion-statement style.

Bailey's Shopping Center
Periwinkle Way and Tarpon Bay Road, Sanibel
(813) 472-1111

SCISSORS

This is a full-service salon that features Matrix hair care products and the latest in haircuts and styles.

1200 Periwinkle Way, Sanibel
(813) 472-5699

Business Needs

ARUNDEL'S HALLMARK SHOPPE

Local, state, national and international packing and shipping service with pickup and delivery, cartons and gift wrapping. Fax, Federal Express and UPS services.

Heart of the Island Shopping Plaza,
1626 Periwinkle, Sanibel
(813) 472-0434 or (813) 472-0430;
Fax number: (813)472-8517

Chadwick's Circle, unit one
(at South Seas Plantation), Captiva.
(813) 395-0434;
Fax number: (813) 395-0981

PAK 'N' SHIP

Packing and shipping services, cartons, Federal Express and UPS.

2402 Palm Ridge Road, Sanibel
(813) 395-1220

PRINT SHOP OF THE ISLANDS

Quick printing, copies and Fax services.

2400 Palm Ridge Road, Sanibel
(813) 472-4592

BIG RED Q QUICK PRINT

Photocopies and all printing needs.

Tree Tops Centre
1101 Periwinkle Way, D #104, Sanibel
(813) 472-2121

PJ'S OFFICE SUPPLIES

Rubber stamps, signs, photocopies;
free delivery.
1624 Periwinkle Way, Sanibel (813) 472-2995

Dry Cleaners and Laundromats

ISLAND DRY CLEANERS & LAUNDROMATS

Bailey's Shopping Center, Tarpon Bay Road &
Periwinkle Way, Sanibel. (813) 395-0055

One-Stop Shops

BAILEY'S GENERAL STORE

Although there are many small grocery stores
on the islands, Bailey's is an institution. It's
been in business since 1899, and it's truly a
general store operated the way they were
nearly 100 years ago. All under one roof you
will find a grocery with a deli section, a hardware store, a bakery and a pharmacy — the
corner drug store moved in from the corner.
They also have 24-hour photo processing
services, men's and women's clothing and fishing tackle and bait.
Bailey's Shopping Center, 2477 Periwinkle Way,
Tarpon Bay Road & Periwinkle Way, Sanibel
Main store (813) 472-1516;
Pharmacy (813) 472-4149

Photography Supplies

ARUNDEL'S

Two prime locations for photography buffs. They use Kodak Royal paper, have one-hour processing and enlargement services, as well as all the supplies you need for plenty of shots on your vacation. While you're there you might want to pick up a card for someone special at the Hallmark card section. They also have a pack-and-ship service if you need to get something somewhere fast and easy.

1626 Periwinkle Way, Sanibel; (813) 472-0434
Chadwick's Square #20, Captiva; (813) 395-0434

MOTOPHOTO

A portrait studio with one-hour photo service, one-hour enlargements, same day E-6 slide service and just about everything under the sun you might need from a photo shop.

Jerry's Plaza,
700 Periwinkle Way, Sanibel
(813) 472-4424

Taxis and Other Transportation

SANIBEL ISLAND TAXI

Regular customers call before they depart on their flights into the Fort Myers Airport for owner J.P. (Pat) Hanley to be there when they arrive. He has an exclusive franchise with the city and is considered a specialist in airport service. The cabs run 24 hours a day and support organizations such as MADD (Mothers Against Drunk Driving) and TADD (Taxis Against Drunk Driving).

695 Tarpon Bay Road #6, Sanibel
(813) 472-4160

SANIBEL LIMOUSINE

You can ride in style around town, downtown, out of town, all the way to Miami for shopping or enjoying its multicultural night life.
(813) 472-8888

TROLLEY TOURS

The trackless trolleys depart from the Chamber of Commerce Visitor Center at the entrance to the islands. The schedule shifts in the off-months, so telephone to check the times and pickup points if you're not

visiting November through May. Round-trip
fares with unlimited reboarding privileges are
available as are all-day tickets. There is also
a two-hour narrated tour of "History and
More," departing from the Visitor Center at
10 a.m. and 12:30 p.m. on Monday,
Wednesday and Fridays. It offers a terrific
overview of these special places in the sun.

Sanibel-Captiva
(813) 472-6374

WATER TAXI SHUTTLE

One price per person gets you a round-trip
tour of the area. Call ahead for reservations
and information on times and destinations.

Captain Marc Brilhat, North Captiva
(813) 395-8377 or (813) 395-0826

SANIBEL TAXI AND AIRPORT SHUTTLE

(813) 472-0007

FUN IN THE SUN

Beaches

THERE ARE 14 MILES OF SHELL-STREWN SANDS ON the islands, and the inviting teal and azure-blue waters beckon as soon as you pass the tollbooth and begin to cross the causeway. Pull over and park for a spell to splash and soak up the rays while planning your attack. If you're heading for South Seas Plantation or the other resorts large and small, you no doubt have brochures in hand and know what to expect from their beachfront locations. But if you're a day-tripper or staying off the beach — although "off the beach" is not very easy to do in these water-surrounded islands in the sun — you'll need the time to look at maps and add to the anticipation.

As you leave the last finger of causeway pointing the way to your escape, turn left and follow Periwinkle Way to the beaches at the southeast tip of Sanibel. Lighthouse Park, named for the silent sentinel towering over the sand, pine and palms at Point Ybel, has five acres of undeveloped beach. Close by on both the Gulf of Mexico and San Carlos Bay is Sanibel Beach, at Seagrape and Buttonwood streets. Dixie Beach, north of Buttonwood, is on the bay, as is the Sanibel Fishing Pier.

There's also a half-mile of undeveloped beach called Flowing Well located off Beach Road, Nerita, Donax and Falgur streets near the point of the promontory. The largest beach is the 30-acre Gulfside City Park at Algiers Beach, accessed by Southwinds Drive East. Like the other beaches, all of which are free, there are parking spaces and restrooms, but no showers. Unlike the other stretches of sand, there are lifeguards and concession stands.

Bowman's Beach is at the north end of Sanibel with clearly marked access from Sanibel-Captiva Road, and farther north, at the southern end of Captiva, is the three-acre Turner Beach, accessed by the same road.

Shelling

WELCOME TO THE CAPITAL OF CONCHS AND CONES,
drills and whelks, the finest selection of shells
on the continent, the third-greatest place
in the world to collect all those chitinous-
covered homes of crawlers and swimmers of
the briny deep. If you want to get technical,
check with the experts and learn all about
such tongue-twisting terms as echinoderms
and polyzoans, the cuttlebone of the
argonauts and the exoskeletal integuments of
the crustaceans. Look for key definitions
of the ornamentation, the mantle and varix,
imbrications, knobs, nodules, spines and
straie, all to describe the unique configura-
tions formed by homes of a wide variety of
invertebrates. You can find the manuals with
all the facts and figures and a great many illustrations and photographs, but if you don't
want a degree in conchology, if you just want
to be a little bit of an expert, or if you merely
want to be able to tell your friends back home
what it is you have on the coffee table, pick
up less complicated publications at one of the
islands' excellent bookstores (see page 106).
Take the crash course, Shell Collecting 101,
and learn how to identify periwinkle and
lion's paw, spiny jewel box, banded tulip,
coquina, turkey wings and sunray Venus.

The shell shops of Sanibel can also provide books and a hands-on introduction. You can supplement your own efforts by purchasing some of the real beauties — remembering to tell all your friends who ooh and aah over your good fortune that you bought them and did not pluck them from the sand during your very own Sanibel stoop.

Webster defines the noun stoop as the act of stooping; a habitual forward bend of the back and shoulders; and as a descent from dignity or superiority; condescension; an act or position of submission, concession. Yes! All of the above fits when you stoop to conquer and collect your share of the shells, wondering about all the other stoopers, including the really dedicated ones who are out long before dawn, outfitted with flashlights or miner's caps with beaming illumination. You'll see them at the prime shelling spots, such as Bowman's Beach, an emerged sandbar, and at Blind Pass, underneath and alongside the bridge that connects the two islands. The best time to stoop is in the winter season, particularly during the months of January and February when Gulf storms, especially those that blow in from the Northwest, sweep in shells by the thousands.

A word of warning about the collection of live shells. Island conservationists and officials believe in strict enforcement of the Florida State Department of Natural Resources' Marine

Fisheries Conservation Rules. They limit the
taking of live shells of any species to two per
person. Violators are subject to a $500 fine
and 60 days in jail — and that's for the first
offense!

A word of welcome from the veteran
Sanibel Stoopers, those friendly folk who have
been organizing an annual Sanibel Shell Fair
since the days of Lindbergh and Darling in
1937. The first week in March is when conchologists and casual collectors, tourists and
dealers, rally from around the globe to display
their wares, to buy and sell, and to compete
for the prizes. They're given for Best Shell in
the Show, Best Exhibit, Best Flower
Arrangement of Shells and Best Christmas
Themes in Shells, and are awarded at a grand
banquet held at the Dunes Golf & Tennis
Club's Mulligan's Restaurant. Reservations are
required, so if you want to congregate and
converse with the conchologists, telephone
(813) 936-6044.

Nature Trails and Tours

AQUA TREK, INC.

This is a wonderful half-day marine biology trip that will take you through the grass flats, mangroves and exploration of several beaches and then for a guided tour to their own private oceanarium and 130-gallon touch tank. You are forewarned to be prepared to get wet up to your waist. They provide the wading shoes, you provide your own towels and sunblock. Pickup and drop-off points can be arranged, and transportation is by van.

P.O. Box 1425, Sanibel
(813) 472-8680

J. N. "DING" DARLING NATIONAL WILDLIFE REFUGE

The refuge was named for the Pulitzer Prize-winning cartoonist from the *New York Herald Tribune.* Darling was an enthusiastic winter visitor to the islands and an early environmentalist pushing for preservation and conservation when those subjects were not really in vogue, understood or even of concern. Established in his memory in 1945 by the U.S. Fish and Wildlife Service, the 4,900-acre refuge is home to an abundance of wildlife dependent on the vegetation of the uplands and the mangrove swamp that predominate. There are armadillos and gopher

tortoises, black racers, indigos, coral and other
snakes; rabbits and raccoons and woodland
birds. Wintering waterfowl — blue and green-
winged teals, coots and shovelers, pintails,
scaup and widgeons thrive on the muck and
widgeon grass and other aquatic plants. Then
there are the wading birds in the ponds, canals
and mud flats, the egrets and plovers, willets,
herons, ibis, sanderlings and spoonbills. A
birdwatcher's dream — or nightmare when
one suddenly comes across a gathering of
black and turkey vultures, the garbage men
of the islands feeding on carrion. There's
also an active population of that most per-
sistent of fishermen, the red-shouldered hawk.
Bald eagles also visit the sanctuary seeking
sustenance.

They are all there to be seen by those who
exercise a little patience, those hiking the
six miles of nature trails or taking the five-
mile self-guided drive, stopping at the markers
along the road, originally built as a dike
during the early days of mosquito control.
The Indigo Trail is our favorite. It starts at
the visitor center, which is open daily
and provides a very valuable introduction
with a slide show, to the refuge's natural
habitat.

For those who want to leave the driving to
someone else, there's the Tram Tours of
Tarpon Bay, the licensed concessionaire for

the refuge. They run regular tours led by experienced, knowledgeable guides who will also take you on canoe trips in and around the refuge. Or you can rent your own canoe or bicycle and do it yourself. They're located at the end of Tarpon Bay Road by the water. Telephone for hours and reservations.

(813) 472-8900

SANIBEL-CAPTIVA CONSERVATION FOUNDATION

Most of the 1,200 acres owned by the foundation are located along the Sanibel River. At the headquarters building, classes are taught on conservation, Florida's natural environment and related subjects. In the 240 acres surrounding the headquarters are numerous well-kept nature trails you can tour with a well-trained guide who wears many hats including Education Director, teacher and liaison for the foundation. There is also a narrative boat cruise [(813) 472-7549] , Native Plant Nursery [(813) 472-1932] and gift shop. Why not join them as a member? Ask a volunteer for an application form.

Sanibel-Captiva Road,
(East just past St. Isabel's)
(813) 472-2329

Bicycles, Mopeds and Scooters

BILLY'S BEACH SERVICE

With four locations on the islands you can be sure you will be able to rent just the right ride for each member of the family. They also rent beach chairs, umbrellas, Windsurfers, Sunfish and Hobie Cat catamarans.

Snook Motel, Sundial Beach & Tennis Resort (for guests' use only), 'Tween Waters Inn, West Wind Inn Main number: (813) 472-8717

ISLAND MOPED

Ask for it and they have it: cruisers, 1-, 3-, 10-, and 21-speed mountain and beach bikes. Tandems, trikes, surries (three wheeler with canopy), quadracycles (four wheeler, three passenger) and buddy bikes (side-by-side) are specialty bikes that can be rented. For those who want some power, try the scooters and mopeds. Baby seats (small fee), baskets and locks (free) are also available. If you rent for more than one day, there's free pickup and delivery. Don't forget to pick up your complimentary cyclist guide.

*1470 Periwinkle Way, Sanibel
(813) 472-5248*

JIM'S BIKE AND SCOOTER RENTAL

Located between the Mucky Duck and The Island Store, this bike shop is in a great spot, and the rentals are reasonably priced.

11534 Andy Rosse Lane, Captiva
(813) 472-1296

THE BIKE RENTAL, INC.

Rent the wheels of your choice for an hour, a week or a month. They have 1-, 3-, and 10-speed; Cross 3- and 5-speed trail, tandem, adult trike, pro all-terrain and road bikes. Baby seats for a small fee; cable, lock and basket loaners are available.

2330 Palm Ridge Road, Sanibel
(813) 472-2241

Tennis and Golf

BEACHVIEW GOLF CLUB

Originally a nine-hole course opened in 1976, this 18-hole, par 70 course with a beautiful setting along the Sanibel River is open to the public. Carts are available.

1100 Par View Drive, Sanibel
(813) 472-2626

THE DUNES GOLF AND TENNIS CLUB & TERRY'S TENNIS SHOP

The fully stocked pro shop has racquets, shoes and clothing for the courts, racquet restringing — everything you need for the game, including lessons from a tennis pro. Whether you're a beginner who's been wanting to learn the game, or an experienced player who just wants to improve your serve, you can take lessons from a private instructor or at the clinic. They also have racquet and ball machine rentals.

The 18-hole 5,600-yard, par 70 course was designed by Mark McCumber and is a water-dotted delight for the sure-handed, precision shot-maker. The 18th hole is a real zinger!

949 Sand Castle Road, Sanibel
(813) 472-2535, (813) 472-3522
Clubhouse: (813) 472-3355

Cruises, Boat Rentals, Wave Runners and Jet Skis

ADVENTURE SAILING CHARTERS

Bring the whole family! Up to six people can enjoy a whole- or half-day tour sailing the beautiful waters of Sanibel-Captiva. Or you can schedule a glorious sunset sail, and watch the brilliance of the sun as it sinks into the horizon. In business since 1976, Captain Mike McMillan promises smooth sailing.

South Seas Plantation Marina, Captiva
(813) 472-7532, days; (813) 472-4386, nights

AIMEE B

This 32-foot Nordic with enclosed cabin, air conditioning and head, is one of the most comfortable vessels in the area for fishing, shelling, sightseeing, nature trips and luncheons. It's available for private or shared charters.

Captain Ralph Bartholomew, (813) 472-5277

CANOE ADVENTURES

Three canoe trips are available with destinations to Sanibel River, Buck Key or "Ding" Darling Wildlife Refuge. If you stay in the area long enough you may want to try all three.

Bird Westall, (813) 472-5218

CAPTAIN JOE BURNSED

Plan a trip snorkeling, sightseeing, lunching, shelling and fishing on the 25-foot center console with a native Florida guide who knows the area.

Castaways Marina, 6460 Sanibel-Captiva Road, Sanibel. (813) 472-8658, (813) 395-0214

CAPTAIN JON CARPENITO

Aside from the exciting night fishing for sharks, six-hour charters going after the big tarpon, or hooking trout, snook, redfish and grouper, you can have a great time on the dinner and sightseeing cruises, trips to isolated Cabbage Key and a joyride on a Booze Cruise. The captain of this 25-foot hydrasport has one motto — "A Good Time Plus a Tan!"

Duzzi Boats Too, (813) 466-6232

CAPTAIN DAVE GIBSON

If fly-fishing the back country and shallow grass flats for tarpon, redfish, trout, snook and even shark is your thing, schedule a charter with Captain Gibson. He's also a light tackle specialist in the sport fishing category. If you just want to sightsee — keeping watch for dolphin, eagles and manatees — or go shelling on North Captiva, Cayo Costa or Johnson Shoals, he can handle that, too, as well as snorkeling trips. He gives a mean lesson in fishin' for those of us beginners who haven't a clue what fish really want. But the main reason to check this guy out is because his sign says "Guaranteed Fun."

(813) 466-4680

CAPTAIN BETTY REED

Her six-hour charter is guaranteed to keep your interest. You can choose snorkeling, shelling, sightseeing or all of the above. A lunch stop is available for those who need refueling. Her motto is "It's a shell of a trip."

(813) 472-4547

CALYPSO CHARTERS

Shelling and sightseeing, fishing, snorkeling and scuba diving with all the equipment on a 27-foot cabin cruiser. Half- or full-day trips are available.

P.O. Box 411, Captiva
(813) 472-1072; (813) 278-2827, voice pager

CLUB NAUTICO

Half- and full-day power boat rentals on 20- to 23-foot Wellcraft with VHF radios, Bimini tops, depth finders, and all the safety equipment needed for a safe and productive trip on Gulf waters or back country.

(813) 472-7540

CAPTAIN BOB SABATINO

Nicknamed "Ol' Man on the Gulf," Cap'n
Bob is quite a character with a solid reputation
for knowing tides, phases of the moon and
how to track down the best fishing holes. His
30 years of experience have filled him with
some exciting and interesting tales, which he
spins aboard his 24½-foot *Privateer*.

(813) 472-7540

CAPTAIN CHUCK SKINNER

Fish in comfort on the *Jeanne Louise* with its
air conditioning and microwave oven. It's the
only Sportfisherman in the area that specializes
in offshore deep-sea adventures. The shark is
the captain's favorite fish to stalk, but he'll
gladly go for anything the passengers want to
catch that day.

Jeanne Louise, Sanibel Island Marina
634 N. Yachtsman Drive, Sanibel
(813) 335-6898; (813) 335-6898, beeper

PIECES OF EIGHT DIVE CENTER

This is the one-stop-shop for diving enthusi-
asts. Buy or rent all equipment needed to
snorkel or dive, plus cameras, Nikonos lenses,
metal detectors and spear guns. Charter the
30-foot *Island Hopper* for a tour of Sanibel-
Captiva. It holds 18 passengers and has an
on-board cooler.

South Seas Plantation, Captiva
(813) 472-9424, in-house extension 3448

FISHY BUSINESS CHARTERS

Half- and full-day charters and split trips are available. All equipment is included, so pack that cooler and go fishin'.

Captain Randy Barfield
(813) 472-2628, (813) 472-BOAT

GAMEFISHER CHARTERS

Call day or night to schedule a four-, six-, or eight-hour charter fishing the Gulf or bay waters and going after tarpon, grouper, redfish, snook, trout, or even shark. Or shell and sightsee on the many little islands in surrounding waters. Recommended by locals, Captain Fussell is one of the leading fishermen in the area.

Captain John Fussell
Sanibel Island Marina
635 N. Yachtsman Drive, Sanibel
(813) 267-6444

JANICE TOO CHARTERS

With 25-plus years experience fishing in area waters and a boat that is tournament rigged, you'll be sure to catch one worth bragging about. Captain Dominic knows the best shelling and sightseeing destinations. Call for reservations.

Captain Dominic, (813) 472-9155

JENSEN'S TWIN PALM RESORT & MARINA

Rent a boat and go out on your own at your
own pace. Drive the waters of the Gulf to
sightsee, fish or wait for the sunset on one of
the remote beaches.

P.O. Box 191
15107 Captiva Drive, Captiva
(813) 472-5800

MOTOR LAUNCH CRUISES

Go shelling, sightseeing or cruising on 90-
minute tours that take you out for dolphin,
bird and sunset-watching.

Sanibel Island Marina, 634 Yachtsman Drive, Sanibel
(813) 472-2531

SUPER FEAT PARASAILING AND
WATER SKI SCHOOL

You choose how long and how high (five, 10
or 15 minutes; 300, 450, 600 feet) to fly.
That tells owner Randy Filter how many dips
you can handle, if you want to free fall like a
real parachute jumper, and whether or not
you want to be pulled back up after the free
fall. Pickup is usually on the beach, but he
will pick you up almost anywhere in the
island area. Life preservers are always worn.

North end of main road on Sanibel at the public beach
(813) 283-2020

YOLO WATER SPORTS

YOLO, as in You Only Live Once, is where you arrange for para-sailing in Captiva, soaring 500 to 550 feet in the air on 8-, 12- (one dip) and 18-minute (two dips) rides, from a boat named *Splash Mary on the Dash,* commanded by Captain Marcel, who operates out of brother Jim's Bike and Scooter Rental shop (see page 86).

11534 Andy Rosse Lane, Captiva
(813) 472-1296

WINDSURFING OF SANIBEL

Group rates are available as well as private lessons and your choice of standard or high-performance boards.

1554 Periwinkle Way, Sanibel
(813) 472-5111, extension 3456

Fishing Equipment

THE BAIT BOX

Known as the island fisherman's headquarters, with combined staff experience of more than 100 years. It's hard to go wrong when buying, renting or having equipment repaired. You can also be confident you'll get the best advice on frozen and live bait, protective gear and maybe a tip about where to cast for the big ones.

1041 Periwinkle Way, Sanibel
(813) 472-1618

OFFSHORE NAUTICAL

This is the best place on the islands to get marine electronics at a good price. If you're going after the big ones you'll need some navigation equipment and radios to keep in touch with the mainland. Captain Jerry knows his stuff, and he arranges for installation. If he doesn't have it in stock, he'll order it.

Periwinkle Gardens, 1551 Periwinkle Way, Sanibel
(813) 472-2224

Marinas

CASTAWAYS MARINA

The boat slips and launch ramp are for guests only, but this is the home dock of many boat captains with rigs for half- and full-day charters.

6460 Sanibel-Captiva Road, Sanibel
(813) 472-1112

JENSEN'S TWIN PALMS RESORT AND MARINA

The docks are in Roosevelt Channel and can accommodate up to 20 boats. There is also a water taxi operation here that offers marine trips to the outer islands.

15107 Captiva Drive, Captiva
(813) 472-4800

SANIBEL HARBOR MARINA

There is a ship's store plus marine parts department, and dry storage for boats as well as six charters operating out of here.

15051 Punta Rassa Road, Sanibel Causeway, Sanibel
(813) 454-0141

SANIBEL ISLAND MARINA

Buy your own boat or rent a power or pontoon boat then stock up on supplies at the ship's store. You can also charter a fishing or sightseeing trip and leave the driving to the experienced captains.

634 North Yachtsman Drive, Sanibel
(813) 472-2723

TIMMY'S NOOK MARINA

If you're planning a fishing excursion you can get your bait and tackle at the shop here. They have the lures and live bait for backcountry or Gulf fishing and can give you some tips on where to go and what to use.

1583 Captiva Drive, Captiva
(813) 472-9444

FUN OUT OF THE SUN

Lounges and Nightclubs

CHADWICK'S

Live entertainment at Chadwick's lounge
varies from Big Band to rock 'n' roll and
country Wednesday through Monday
evenings. On Tuesdays you can enjoy a steel
drum band.

At the entrance to South Seas Plantation, Captiva
(813) 472-5111

CROW'S NEST LOUNGE

The locals say this is the No. 1 nightspot on
the island with live entertainment and dancing Tuesday through Sunday, and live crab
races on Monday. They serve fun and food
starting just before noon, and have an evening
happy hour with reduced drink prices daily.

'Tween Waters Inn, Captiva Drive, Captiva
(813) 472-5161

McT'S SHRIMP HOUSE & TAVERN

Stick around after dinner and enjoy the informal atmosphere of this neighborhood tavern while you play darts, video games, watch the big screen TV or entertain family and friends at the nightly Karaoke Party. The Key lime daiquiris are delicious.

1523 Periwinkle Way, Sanibel
(813) 472-3161

PATIO LOUNGE

Dinner and dancing take on new meaning here with reggae on Saturdays and Sundays, dance music Mondays, Tuesdays, Thursdays and Fridays, and Dixieland jazz on Wednesdays.

The Jacaranda, 1223 Periwinkle Way, Sanibel
(813) 472-1771

WIL'S LANDING

During dinner you can enjoy the soft piano music Tuesday through Saturday, but things liven up after dinner on Friday and Saturday nights when the band plays dance tunes to move to 'til midnight.

1200 Periwinkle Way, Sanibel
(813) 472-4772

Movies

ISLAND CINEMA

This one-screen theater is open evenings and features first-run movies. Call for show times.

Bailey Shopping Center
Tarpon Bay Road, Sanibel
(813) 472-1701

Theaters

THE PIRATE PLAYHOUSE

A professional equity theater opened in 1991 across Periwinkle Way from the Community Center. The season, featuring the likes of *The Boys Next Door* and *Dracula*, runs from November through April.

The old Pirate Playhouse, which performed in the former Sanibel Elementary School built in 1894, was going to be torn down a couple of years ago, and so the company built the new theater. However, the preservationists prevailed once again; the building was saved, and other theater groups perform in the historic schoolhouse.

2200 Periwinkle Way, Sanibel
(813) 472-0006

Museums

THE ISLAND HISTORICAL MUSEUM

There are not too many surviving structures
from the "good" old days, so this tin-roofed
Florida Cracker farmhouse, raised on concrete
pillars to let flood waters flow through (not to
shade and shelter snakes as some of the old-
timers would have you believe), is a real
treasure. The home was built in 1913 from
termite-impervious Dade County pine on
land homesteaded by Pastor Andrew Wiren, a
retired minister from New Sweden, Maine,
who arrived on Sanibel the year the lighthouse
was built. The farmhouse was moved to this
site next to the Sanibel City Hall in 1982 to
serve as a most suitable home of the Historical
Preservation Committee's Historical Museum.
The kitchen has been upgraded a bit over the
years, but otherwise the home gives a time
capsule peek into the lifestyle of the rugged
pioneers. The museum is open Wednesday
through Saturday 10 a.m to 4 p.m.

900 Dunlop Road, Sanibel
(813) 472-4648

THE BAILEY-MATTHEWS SHELL MUSEUM

A long-lasting dream of the dedicated shellers
of Sanibel, this all-encompassing museum,
when it is finished, will be devoted to the
seashell in all its myriad and marvelous forms.
There will be separate sections covering the
lore and history, and all the expert material
and reference works a conchologist could
want. It is being built on a splendid eight-acre
site donated by the heirs of the Baileys — as
in Bailey's Corner and Bailey's General Store
and Bailey's Shopping Center. The nonprofit
organization in charge is The Shell Museum
& Educational Foundation, Inc., and they
have established a preview office.

(813) 395-2233

Art Galleries

ABORIGINALS: ART OF THE FIRST PERSON

Fine tribal art from Aboriginal Australia, Africa Oceania and Native America is featured here.

2340 Periwinkle Way, Sanibel
(813) 395-2200

CHIARINO GALLERY

Check out the sophisticated and unusual sculptures and gifts in this gallery.

Periwinkle Place
2075 Periwinkle Way, 2nd Floor, #24 West, Sanibel
(813) 395-0444

DOLPHIN WATERS

This marine life art gallery is filled with depictions of life from the sea captured in bronze, wood, ceramic, glass and on print. Dolphins, tropical fish, turtles and manatees are some of the subjects.

Timbers Plaza, 707 Tarpon Bay Road, Sanibel
(813) 472-4688

EL CONDOR MARKETPLACE

Filled with folk art, ethnic jewelry, home accessories and apparel, this gallery doubles as a boutique and a wonderful place for buying gifts.

2359 Periwinkle Way, Sanibel
(813) 472-0433

THE FOUNDERS GALLERY AND
THE PHILLIPS GALLERY

Twelve years ago, a small group of local artists, hoping to make Sanibel and Captiva the "island of the arts," formed the Barrier Island Group for the Arts (BIG Arts) and opened these two galleries. The galleries, joined by a large breezeway, feature paintings by Florida artists. The Phillips gallery is also the setting for musical events, classes and workshops.

900 Dunlop Road, Sanibel
(813) 395-0900

ISLAND WILDLIFE GALLERY

Local artists bring their wood, brass, bronze, copper and paper sculptures to life recreating the animals of the area and capturing them in photographs and other artistic medium.

2640 Palm Ridge Road, Corner of Palm Ridge and Tarpon Bay Road, Sanibel
(813) 395-1100

JUNGLE DRUMS

Nature art in the form of jewelry, paintings, sculptures and home accessories.

11532 Andy Rosse Lane (before the Mucky Duck)
P.O. Box 368, Captiva
(813) 395-2266

LIVING ARTS

Everything is crafted in the U.S. in this contemporary gallery with jewelry, pottery, wind chimes, bells, glass and porcelain.

Periwinkle Gardens
1551 Periwinkle Way, Sanibel
(813) 472-0035

SAGEBRUSH GALLERY

You can find all types of Native American artwork in the form of pottery, sculptures and rugs.

The Village Shops
2340 Periwinkle Way, Sanibel
(813) 472-6971

SCHOOLHOUSE GALLERY

This gallery is owned by Joseph Pulitano, an artist who specializes in abstracts. Most of the art on display are originals done in oils and watercolors by locally and nationally known artists such as Carol Seabold, David Grey and Carl Nelson. They also carry mobiles and sculptures by Arthur Bowman.

520 Tarpon Bay Road, Sanibel
(813) 472-1193; (813) 472-8311

SANIBEL GALLERY

Works of art such as paintings, sculpture and fine crafts created by local and nationally acclaimed artists. Custom framing is available.

Heart of the Island Plaza
1628 Periwinkle Way, Sanibel
(813) 472-3307

TIN CAN ALLEY GALLERY

This gallery, owned by artist Bryce McNamara, carries unusual items such as tables, lamps, lanterns and masks from areas as distant as Guatemala and Kenya.

2480 Library Way, Sanibel
(813) 472-2902

TREEHOUSE GALLERY AND GIFT SHOP

Local artisans create unique forms of art using materials from the area.

630 Tarpon Bay Road, Suite 10, Olde Sanibel
(813) 472-1850

Bookstores and Libraries

THE ISLAND BOOK NOOK

New and used books are available here, and they have a paperback exchange program. Owner Joan Simonds will order any book you want.

2330 Palm Ridge Place, Sanibel
(813) 472-6777

MACINTOSH BOOK SHOP

Established by William MacIntosh shortly after he arrived from Scotland in 1960, this is the island's oldest bookstore. It was originally in another location for two years but has become an island institution in this new setting. The store has a large selection of books, a children's alcove and a great variety of other items available — music cassettes, greeting cards and charts.

2365 Periwinkle Way, Sanibel
(831) 472-1447

SANIBEL ISLAND BOOKSHOP

Stocks everything from best sellers to classics to children's books. There are sections on business, and a wonderful nature room. They have more than 10,000 books in stock.

955 Rabbit Road, Sanibel
(813) 472-5223

CAPTIVA MEMORIAL LIBRARY

Chapin and Wiles, Captiva
(813) 472-2133

SANIBEL PUBLIC LIBRARY

Corner of Palm Ridge Road and Library Way, Sanibel
(813) 472-2483

Festivals and Fairs

BARRIER ISLAND GROUP FOR THE ARTS & CRAFTS FAIR

This juried art show, held during Thanksgiving weekend at the Sanibel Community Center, features the work of artists from across the country.

LUMINARY TRAIL

Sanibel Island lights up during the first week in December when shopkeepers and residents display hundreds of votive candles set in decorative paper bags. Restaurants stay open late for this holiday event.

SANIBEL-CAPTIVA LIONS CLUB ARTS & CRAFTS SHOW

Held the last weekend in March at the Sanibel Community Center, the show features artists and craftspeople from across the country.

SANIBEL JAZZ ON THE GREEN

This festival features the best of jazz and cuisine from area restaurants. It's held the second weekend in October at the Dunes Golf and Tennis Club.

SANIBEL MUSIC FESTIVAL

This popular festival started in the early 1980s when Marilyn Lauriente, part-time Sanibel resident and principal clarinetist of the Chicago Lyric Opera Orchestra, invited some of her fellow musicians to perform on the islands. Lauriente died in 1991, but the festival's devoted board of directors has kept the tradition alive. Chicago musicians typically perform eight concerts during March. Tickets can be purchased in advance, and subscriptions are available.

P.O. Box 1623, Sanibel 33957
October through May phone (813) 395-1375

SANIBEL ROTARY CLUB ARTS & CRAFTS SHOW

Held in February at the Sanibel Recreation Complex, this show attracts regional artists and exhibitors.

SANIBEL SHELL FAIR

Held every spring since 1937 — at the Sanibel Community Center — usually during the first weekend in March, the fair features scientific displays from around the world, shell craft displays, rare shells, and live shell exhibits from local elementary school children.

TASTE OF THE ISLANDS

Held the last weekend in April at the Dunes Golf and Tennis Club, 25 or more area restaurants participate in this food fest.

TUDOR WATCH OCEAN TO OCEAN MISTRAL NATIONAL CHAMPIONSHIP

A windsurfing competition held the second week of November, when some 250 or more multicolored sails fill the Gulf of Mexico to compete for the championship title. The starting place is San Carlos Bay on the Sanibel Causeway.

Index

About the Author

For more than a quarter-century Robert Tolf has been traveling the state of Florida by foot, car, train, boat and plane. A prolific writer with more than 30 books to his credit, he is the restaurant critic and featured travel columnist for the Fort Lauderdale *Sun-Sentinel* and restaurant editor of *Florida Trend* magazine.